Adventures In Changes, Transitions, And Deaths

Primer for Life's Minor and Major Challenges and Passages

KEYS TO
CONSCIOUSNESS AND SURVIVAL
SERIES
Volume 2

Dr. Angela Brownemiller

PRIMER FOR LIFE'S MINOR AND MAJOR CHALLENGES AND PASSAGES

ADVENTURES IN CHANGES, TRANSITIONS, AND DEATHS

Adventures In Changes, Transitions, And Deaths

Primer for Life's Minor and Major Challenges and Passages

KEYS TO
CONSCIOUSNESS AND SURVIVAL
SERIES
Volume 2

Dr. Angela Brownemiller

Metaterra® Publications

Metaterra® Publications
Adventures in Changes, Transitions, and Deaths:
Primer for Life's Minor and Major Challenges and Passages
KEYS TO CONSCIOUSNESS AND SURVIVAL SERIES,
Volume 2
Copyright © 2023, 2024, and 1998, 1999, 2000, 2005, 2010, 2013, 2015, 2020, 2021, 2022
Angela Brownemiller / Angela Browne-Miller / Metaterra® Publications.
All rights reserved in all formats and in
all languages and dialects known or not known at this time.
Published in the United States by Metaterra® Publications.
Library of Congress Cataloging-in-Publication Data.
Brownemiller, Angela.
Adventures in Changes, Transitions, and Deaths
Metaterra/Angela Brownemiller/ 1st Edition., 2nd Edition.
1. Consciousness. 2. Spiritual. 3. Addiction. 4. Recovery.
5. Psychology. 6. Biology. 7. Death and Dying. 8. Future. 9. Trauma.
10. Survival. 11. Consciousness.
12. Angela Brownemiller. 13. Angela Browne-Miller.
14. Dr. Angela. 15. Dr. Angela®
ISBN-13: 978-1-937951-26-9
(Paperback on Amazon).
Also see Amazon and website below for Ebook and Audiobook.
Published in the United States of America for US and worldwide distribution,
by and copyright © Angela Brownemiller.
Cover and content: all illustrations, charts, diagrams, all content and all text,
by and copyright ©Angela Brownemiller.
Book and cover design by and copyright ©Angela Brownemiller.
Ordering information and bulk ordering information available through:
Amazon Paperback and Amazon Kindle and Amazon Audible Audiobook.
All rights to all copies, printings, forms, formats, editions, adaptations, and excerpts reserved. Without prior written and signed permission from the publisher, copyright holder, author, and illustrator, no part of this book (words, text, art, illustrations, diagrams, charts, or other) may be published, and or reproduced, copied, transcribed, distributed, transmitted, broadcast, and or stored, in any form and or by any means, (handwritten, typed, printed, spoken, taped, digital, audio, video, movie, and or other past, present, and or future forms and formats). The exception to this rights restriction is only for the inclusion of a brief (20 to 30 word) quotation (credited to this book, author, illustrator, and publisher).
Thank you.

ADVENTURES IN CHANGES, TRANSITIONS, AND DEATHS

Dedicated to

Evacheska
and
Lee

PRIMER FOR LIFE'S MINOR AND MAJOR CHALLENGES AND PASSAGES

ADVENTURES IN CHANGES, TRANSITIONS, AND DEATHS

Table Of Contents

Dedication	5
Come Fly With The Phoenix:	
You Can Make A Comeback	11
1. Introduction To Change, Transition, Death	15
IMPORTANT NOTE	35
2. The Apocalypse Syndrome	37
3. Physical Death As A Model	55
4. Allowing One's Patterning To Die	81
5. Death And Transcendence	101
6. Mapping Your Transitions And Deaths	129
7. Transitions From	
One Dimension Of Your Reality To Another	149
8. The LEAP Of Faith In Your SELF	159
9. Conceiving Of Personal Dimensions	173
10. Shedding Your Skin	193
11. Harvesting Your Transition And Death Processes	207
12. From Personal Apocalypse Into Power	219
EPILOGUE: Revolution And Death	237
APPENDICES	**261**
Booklist And Recommended Reading	263
Metaterra® Publications	270
About The Author	271

PRIMER FOR LIFE'S MINOR AND MAJOR CHALLENGES AND PASSAGES

ADVENTURES IN CHANGES, TRANSITIONS, AND DEATHS

Figures

Seeing The Light Flowing In To the Valley Of Death   10

Figure 3.1. Overlapping Levels Of Perceived Consciousness   76
Figure 3.2. Our Many Bodies   77
Figure 3.3. Coordinating Biological And Other-Based Death   78
Figure 3.4. The Three Deaths   79

Figure 5.1. Struggle   101
Figure 5.2. Paradox   114
Figure 5.3. Insight   116
Figure 5.4. Elevation   117
Figure 5.5. Adventures In Transcendence   119
Figure 5.6. Struggle Paradox Struggle Paradox   120
Figure 5.7. Struggle And Paradox Into Elevation   121

Figure 6.1. Four Repeatable And Intermixable Phases   130
Figure 6.2. The Fork In The Road   132
Figure 6.3. No Exit Paradox Energy Trap   134
Figure 6.4. The Release   136
Figure 6.5. Death Release Map   145
Figure 6.6. Untrained Death Release Map   146
Figure 6.7. Energy Loss Map   147
Figure 6.8. Profound Release Map   148

Note on Chapter 9 Figures: 174-178
    The figures in this chapter are not numbered as these are distributed throughout the text of this chapter. Please see the pages of this chapter to see these interrelated very sequential figures as one multi-page graphic.

PRIMER FOR LIFE'S MINOR AND MAJOR CHALLENGES AND PASSAGES

Seeing the LIGHT flowing in
to the Valley of Death

ADVENTURES IN CHANGES, TRANSITIONS, AND DEATHS

COME FLY WITH THE PHOENIX
You Can Make a Comeback

It is never too late ... even if you find yourself struggling in the rubble of broken dreams.

You may have been there a moment, a month, a decade – however long. You may feel your pain, your tears, your sense of loss and hopelessness, or you may just feel confusion, or you may just feel nothing at all.

You look for, pray for, hope. You may say please, please someone fix this. Please please show me a way out. Please please God, if you are out there, help me.

The bits and pieces of the life you wanted to lead lie around you, shattered. Everywhere you see wasteland, your own personal wasteland.

PRIMER FOR LIFE'S MINOR AND MAJOR CHALLENGES AND PASSAGES

You tread carefully through the fragments of your fractured dreams because you hurt when you walk on them, as if they are broken glass and your feet are bare.

Yet, these bits are the ingredients of something new. Put them together, like pieces of a jigsaw puzzle. And you will solve the mystery of the new you. There is a secret there among those ruins, there is something new waiting for you to see.

There is always time to begin the next moment, no matter how brief it may be, again.

A hand reaches out from somewhere, a hand you can almost see. Is this your imagination, or is there someone there? Look again, the hand you see is your own. Yes, there may be others trying to help. Or you may be all alone in this. But the hand you see is your own.

You are calling yourself back to life. Listen. You want to be heard. You want to come back.

There is much to see from this rock bottom place. Sometimes we can see through our tears and fears and

ADVENTURES IN CHANGES, TRANSITIONS, AND DEATHS

distress. This may not be easy. Yet we can look for, may just imagine there is, even a dot, a speck, a bit of light there.

Open your eyes. Follow this light, the idea that there is maybe even just the idea of light, of a sort of life raft, of a kind of hope, out there. Look, just wait and look.

PRIMER FOR LIFE'S MINOR AND MAJOR CHALLENGES AND PASSAGES

ADVENTURES IN CHANGES, TRANSITIONS, AND DEATHS

1
Introduction To
Change, Transition, And Death

> *This chapter introduces the idea that changes, transitions, and endings of many forms are all somewhat like deaths. These are deaths of conditions and situations such as relationships, or stages of life, or behaviors, or other phases and patterns. We can learn about death from in-life situations, and we can learn about processes in our lives by understanding death.*

Adventures In Change, Transition, And Death is written for anyone who is undergoing, has undergone, or will undergo biological death, which is considered by many people to be the *end-of-life* or at least *end-of-biological-life* transition. This book is also written for anyone who is undergoing, has undergone, or will undergo any major *in-life* (even sometimes in *daily life*) ending, change, or transition. Thus, this book is written for everyone.

In-life, yes, even sometimes in daily life, endings, changes, and transitions include just about everything we may experience at some time. This can include divorce, being fired, leaving home or having one's children leave home. This can include abrupt changes or events such as having one's home be damaged in an earthquake, sustaining an injury, or having something precious stolen.

This also can include gradual but definite changes such as: changes in behavioral patterns -- outgrowing a stage of life, growing older, and also processes such as shifting out of a steady or an addictive relationship to a drug, a person, a behavior, or a philosophy. This can also include having old friends die; or, even undergoing the disease process, whether it is temporary, chronic or terminal.

And, of course, we include here the model of death with which we think we are so familiar: physical (biological) death, which is seen by many people as the ultimate of all deaths, the seemingly final death. Indeed, physical

(biological) death itself – and the challenging emotions that can sometimes accompany it -- such as avoidance, denial, anxiety, fear, anger, depression, or maybe confusion, or numbness, or maybe acceptance, or even insight and spiritual elevation – together offer an excellent model for all the minor and major changes, transitions, endings -- that each and every one of us may at some time endure.

Of course, most of the in-life deaths listed above and on the previous pages are not actual biological deaths. Rather, these are experiences that may feel like death, in that situations and patterns are radically changing or even ending.

WHAT WE FEEL WE CAN
ENDURE

The word "endure" is used here in the sense that changes, transitions, endings of various forms, are all deaths of a situation or phase or pattern. And, these minor and major deaths can in some way be navigated, survived -- endured.

Clearly, anxiety and suffering can be difficult experiences to stay positive during. Many Readers know how intensely challenging it can be to stay positive. At times, even the idea of staying positive may sound impossible, irrelevant, ridiculous.

In this book, the idea of staying positive is not simply about putting a smile on your face when you do not feel like smiling.[1] This is more about adding to or expanding your frame of reference, your view of your own self and of your own reality as you find your way through the challenges you may face.

---

[1] Of course, some research indicates that when we put a smile on our face, our brain responds with happy or at least positive-seeming emotions for us to feel. For example, see Neuroscience News, 2020. *Smiling Can Trick Your Mind Into Being More Positive.* https://neurosciencenews.com/smiling-mind-positive-16813/ .

And, on the other hand, many forced smiles are not really smiles, and may show up in times of fear or stress, such as what we find in zoos when animals are afraid or stressed, this being known as the primate fear grimace. For example, see the article titled: *Cheerful Chimps: Are Animals Really Happy When They Smile? A smiling face might not signal what we think, if there's anything to be learned from other primates,* in De Waal, Frans, (2021). *Discover.* Feb. 11.

https://www.discovermagazine.com/planet-earth/cheerful-chimps-are-animals-really-happy-when-they-smile .

ADVENTURES IN CHANGES, TRANSITIONS, AND DEATHS

On some level, in some way, it can be good to tell yourself that you CAN make it through, no matter how impossible "making it through" seems to be, no matter how impossible the transition appears to be. We may want to re-think what "making it through," enduring, actually means.

TELLING YOURSELF
YOU CAN MAKE IT THROUGH,
YOU CAN
SURVIVE

Of course, this can involve your telling yourself what making it through could look like. For example, some people choose to focus on the idea of an after-life so that death seems less final, so that there is something BEYOND.

[And of course, one of the best aspects of this belief in after-life, as I suggest in other of my books in this KEYS TO CONSCIOUSNESS AND SURVIVAL SERIES (such as in the HOW TO DIE AND SURVIVE books) is that we may indeed be able to survive as a consciousness, to learn *how to survive as a consciousness* when moving BEYOND. Once we know,

or believe, that we can learn to do this, learn to survive, we can be actively developing this view of life and death and life BEYOND death -- which is not really death, is it?]

BUILDING YOUR OWN
LIFE RAFT

A sense of a future, a continuity of the SELF, can be a powerful guide. And even any form of hope can be valuable. Even a speck, a shred, a tiny bit of light, of optimism, can be an emotional or spiritual life raft. Survival itself takes on a new meaning.

(See other books in this KEYS TO CONSCIOUSNESS AND SURVIVAL SERIES for more on this matter, and for exercises involved in enduring, in navigating, change, transition, and death processes. Refer to the Recommended Reading List in the APPENDICES Section of this present book, where books such as the HOW TO DIE AND SURVIVE BOOKS are listed.)

On some level, you already know everything said on these pages. You have already been through many

ADVENTURES IN CHANGES, TRANSITIONS, AND DEATHS

profound transitions in your lifetime. (And here, some of you Readers ask me to add: yes, and perhaps in other lifetimes as well.)

WHEN CHALLENGES AND TRYING TIMES CAN YIELD KNOWLEDGE AND EVEN STRENGTH AND EVEN ENERGY

So here you are. You have been born, you have walked your first steps. You probably had a first day of school, became an adolescent, fell in love for the first time, broke up with your first boy or girl friend, finished school, left home, got hired, and maybe have been laid off or fired, perhaps married, divorced, mourned the death of a family member or friend, or have experienced some other life changes.

Of course, not all of these events are considered unpleasant or difficult experiences. And, again most of these are not actual deaths. Why, then, would these events be referred to as deaths of situations, phases, patterns, in this book about change, transition, and death? Because all

PRIMER FOR LIFE'S MINOR AND MAJOR CHALLENGES AND PASSAGES

changes, whether they seem to be so-called "good" or "bad" changes, are types of endings, even deaths. Something is ending or transitioning – or at least trying to.

We must allow ourselves to stretch the meaning of the word "death" this way in order to ever more fully understand and deal with death. This is because even thinking through, let alone going through, the process of death itself can be confusing, or conflicting, or intense, or even tremendously challenging.

Here is where a mild or general or even profound re-thinking of change, transition, and death processes can be useful. Once we understand change and transition processes as forms of death processes, we see how life prepares us more every day to find our way through challenges and even death processes, even biological death processes.

ADVENTURES IN CHANGES, TRANSITIONS, AND DEATHS

IT IS HOW YOU NAVIGATE

Look back on your life. Think of the many experiences you found difficult or painful as they were happening and later saw as "not so bad," useful, maybe even great.

Death, the death of anything -- your marriage, your way of life, your body -- is merely a transition, a passage. It would be dishonest to say that death is not an ending. Death can be defined as an ending AND as a transition into a new beginning.

It is how you define and navigate this transition that will set the stage for your next beginning.

The more you understand the process, the great adventure of change, transition, and death, the more you can use the experience to consciously -- with your full attention at work upon it -- create the next phase of your self, your being, your life -- design your new reality.

Death, in any form, whether in-life changes and endings, or even end-of-life changes and endings, is, indeed a great adventure. In this sense, understanding more about minor and major death situations can be a challenging, wondrous, remarkable journey every time you take it.

THESE PROCESSES ARE LESSONS

No two transitions or deaths are the same; however, the passage we call death has characteristics which can be identified again and again.

Learning to recognize these characteristics, these landmarks along the road of transition, will ease your passage, will enhance the richness of your experience, will further generate your sense of survival (in the form you learn to choose).

This learning can help you define for yourself the characteristics of, even what may be the quality of, the survival -- the richness of the harvest -- you take from your

ADVENTURES IN CHANGES, TRANSITIONS, AND DEATHS

change, transition, and death processes. (See later chapters in this book, such as Chapters 5 and 6, where ways to see patterns and processes of change and transition, even of death, are presented.)

RECOGNIZE AND TAKE YOUR ENERGY

When moving through a change or transition or death, energy that has been locked up in an old pattern can be released. You can become more aware of what this release means, and learn to release your own energy back to yourself. This release of your own energy to yourself can be key in survival.

(Other books in this KEYS TO CONSCIOUSNESS AND SURVIVAL SERIES detail processes of this release. See for example, the NAVIGATING LIFE'S STUFF books and the HOW TO DIE AND SURVIVE books – listed in the Recommended Reading List in the APPENDICES section of this present book.)

YOU CAN TRANSFORM YOUR PROCESS

And you *can* harvest your death for your own energy, for your own SELF.

Even if it is one of the more difficult passages you may undergo during your life on this Earth -- a divorce or other family breakup; a major downturn in financial, career, health, or social status; a physical disaster of some sort; or physical death itself –

**You can transform your experience of
the process
by transforming
your definition of your process.
This is key in the
<u>adventures in change, transition, and death</u>
this book shares.**

You can transform your process, even a challenging process, from what may perhaps be a situation through which you feel to be aimlessly and hopelessly tumbling, into a profound initiation.

ADVENTURES IN CHANGES, TRANSITIONS, AND DEATHS

GREAT INITIATION

Even physical death is a great initiation. On some level we are aware of this. We can be learning about what this means as we live our lives. Even on a daily basis, we are presented with situations that invite us to consciously move through their processes – to learn what it means to ever more consciously move through.

Yet, few people consciously prepare for this initiation-by-death, or for any of their other seemingly smaller initiation-by-living change, transition, and death processes and adventures.

This is because we tend to look away from, or sometimes even be afraid of, great changes, especially when these appear to be great unknowns. So, we do not consciously plan for these, except to buy insurance, write wills, and pray for some kind of salvation or direction. However, it is not only fear which keeps us from preparing for initiation-by-death. Consider these common states of mind that may be affecting our readiness for change,

transition, and death. These are states of mind (and brain) that will be referred to several times in this book:

Fear Is A State Of Mind

Fear is certainly one of the states of mind that can keep us from knowing how to plan for, manage, take control of, successfully endure, and harvest our energy as the patterns affecting us are changing or even dying.

Deep Programming Is A State Of Mind

Next to fear is our deep programming, the behavioral and energetic patterning to which we (our minds, even our brains themselves) are programmed to be patterned, addicted.

Lack Of Information Is A State Of Not-Knowing

And, next to programmed-in pattern addiction is lack of information: We have not been taught the true nature of change, transition, and death processes. We have either denied ourselves or have been denied the truth about these.

ADVENTURES IN CHANGES, TRANSITIONS, AND DEATHS

Group Or Social, Societal, Perception Is A State Of Mind

And, beyond the above listed states of mind is the social state of mind regarding understanding death itself -- the cultural taboos and laws we have developed and enacted against learning how to die well and as consciously as we can, against actually dying a physical death with grace and at will.

[This is <u>not</u> to advocate suicide as an impulsive, desperate way out of the challenges of life. This is, however, to advocate in favor of an adult individual's right to die -- your right to choose for yourself (and for no one but yourself) the time, place, and method of your own death, so long as you are making a responsible choice harming no one.]

YOU CAN HAVE A SAY

You may be able to work with yourself on how you define any emotional and physical confusion, stress, and suffering you may undergo in your changes, transitions,

endings, dyings, physical or otherwise. Of course, this can be difficult when the emotional and or physical pain are so intense that the pain itself may take center stage.

There is such good guidance we can be, or may be, receiving as we live our lives. Yet, we may not have been told we can prepare in advance – whether it be years or moments in advance -- for times when we may need to know how to work with ourselves to navigate situations, changes, transitions, even deaths.

We may not have been shown how to see the patterns we live in and through. We may not have been shown how to, once we detect these patterns, change or heal these patterns, understand what it means to move through these patterns -- to release the energy held in these patterns, our energy, and to send this energy back to ourselves as we move on.

Ask why many people, perhaps all of us, do not know how to truly understand patterns, to see the powerful workings of these patterns. Consider the possibility that we

ADVENTURES IN CHANGES, TRANSITIONS, AND DEATHS

have been denied the truth -- by religions, by political leaders, by those among us who know – yes, even the truth about death itself, let alone about how life offers such great lessons in death processes.

Why deny us truth? Because we are much easier to control if we spend our energy worrying about, avoiding, or denying death. We are much easier to control through our fears, our pattern addictions, and our lacks of information, even our religious and legislative taboos.

Were each and every one of us able to ride personal, social, and global disaster; personal, social, and global apocalypse; personal, social, and global transition and death processes into greater awareness, even into personal strength and power, we would be an ever more resilient people. We would be more powerful as individuals and as a collective life force.

Whatever forces (from within us or outside us) hold us captive will be severely threatened when we become **masters of our own transition and death processes.**

YOUR MASTERY OF
YOUR LIFE PROCESSES AND TRANSITIONS

I am inviting you to become exactly this: a master of your own change, transition, and death processes and experiences. This will enable you to ever more master your life. After all, we are always living and dying. And so is our world. Rethink the concept of death for yourself and for all humanity. Your -- our -- survival, *our freedom*, depends upon the spreading of this awareness.

You will grow to understand this on an ever deeper level. The following ideas about the death process will flow gently into your awareness, into your consciousness, and will allow you to take these as lightly or as profoundly as you wish -- as you feel ready for.

ADVENTURES IN CHANGES, TRANSITIONS, AND DEATHS

Thank you for joining in on this look at *Adventures in Changes, Transitions, and Deaths*. This little book lays the foundation for a profound journey in personal and group awareness both here and BEYOND, for whatever each of us feels the BEYOND may be.

PRIMER FOR LIFE'S MINOR AND MAJOR CHALLENGES AND PASSAGES

ADVENTURES IN CHANGES, TRANSITIONS, AND DEATHS

IMPORTANT NOTE

Let's be clear here. <u>Nothing</u> in this book advocates suicide, or judges suicide. Many persons' suicides are understandably conducted in a state of desperation, or of extreme confusion, or perhaps quite rationally to exit severe pain.

While such desperation, confusion, pain are for so many truly nearly or entirely unbearable, other options must be made ever more available. We must all look for means of reaching people before they choose suicide. Rarely is suicide a consciously, or even spiritually, fully navigated event. When it truly is, then the individual is making clear choices and is fully conscious of the impact of this event upon the self and others.

Various religions have various views on suicide, and it is up to each Reader to choose her or his own approach to suicide. This book does not take a position on either suicide or euthanasia.

*This book does, however, advocate in favor of an adult individual's right to choose her or his own view on these matters — and right to decide how and when to be involved in the process of her or his own death. Each person has the inalienable birthright right to choose for her or him self what sort of death to have, where, when, how, so long as that person is making a **responsible and fully informed choice, and not doing so in isolation**. The matter of responsible choice will be returned to later. **<u>It may take a lifetime to prepare oneself to make a fully responsible and fully informed choice</u>**.*

(NOTE: It may be that the ability to leave the physical body at will without having to "commit suicide" is present within us. Numerous ancient cultures' teachings (as well as some modern day practices, some adapting ancient traditions, others being new models of this), continue to practice this form of self-willed, consciously selected BODY DEPARTURE. Steps describing this and other processes are presented in Volumes 4, 11, and 14 in this series, the HOW TO DIE AND SURVIVE books, ebooks, and audiobooks. See this present book's APPENDICES.)

PRIMER FOR LIFE'S MINOR AND MAJOR CHALLENGES AND PASSAGES

ADVENTURES IN CHANGES, TRANSITIONS, AND DEATHS

2
The Apocalypse Syndrome

This chapter looks at the mystery of death and how the unknowns of death can themselves be daunting. Somehow, not knowing for certain what happens when we die leaves a question, for many people a forever lingering question. However, of course, some decide they know for certain, or nearly for certain, what happens when we die.

However certain or uncertain you may feel about death itself, understanding the effect that even <u>the idea of death</u> has on us can help us find our way through the maze of unknowns, uncertainties, even for some, spoken or unspoken anxieties or fears.

So now, let's see if we are ready to unmask death and see its face. The mask itself may seem surprisingly easy to remove. Yet, behind the mask are other masks, many layers of faces. Close to the surface is the crust of what is frequently labeled as fear.

PRIMER FOR LIFE'S MINOR AND MAJOR CHALLENGES AND PASSAGES

The label, fear, may be an easy way to label this. This term, fear, may be used for something vague and difficult to define, a sort of sensation waiting in the wings or within the halls of our subconscious spaces. Some of this feeling is indeed an unlabeled undefined free-floating yet invisible sensation, generally one that may be frequently and profoundly affecting many people although largely working on a subconscious level – affecting us yet out of our awareness.

Fear is most certainly a powerful and significant state of mind. Yet fear is also a term, almost a catch phrase, for so many emotions and experiences of feelings. Fear is more than a four letter word. Fear can be elusive, can take obvious as well as vague forms. Vague undefined fear can be deceptive. This sort of free floating concern, discomfort, uneasiness, can almost hide from us while affecting us.

Have you ever felt fear? Have you ever been afraid? If so, did you know you were afraid? If so, how did you know? Do you think this was actually fear you were feeling? Have

ADVENTURES IN CHANGES, TRANSITIONS, AND DEATHS

you examined this fear? Can you unpack this fear and find the many elements and aspects of this fear? Whatever this fear really was, was this fear sensation a help or a hindrance to you?

THAT VAGUE FREE FLOATING FEAR-LIKE SENSATION

So, how do we detect the connection between vague anxieties or even fear-like sensations and the idea of death itself? Both explicitly and implicitly, a vague anxiety or fear-like sensation may be almost invisibly connecting itself to the idea of death -- or to the reality of death. Part of mastering the death process is seeing how fear connects itself, weaves itself into the perceptions we may be having.

The more able we are to dialog with ourselves and others about our feelings about and views on death, the more in touch with our processes we can be. The more conscious we can be. We can begin to be ever more aware of what we are experiencing and better navigate our

experiences. Conscious change, transition, and death becomes ever more possible. Surviving transition becomes ever more do-able.

PROTECTIVE AWARENESS VERSUS BLINDING FEAR

Whatever the sort of death or transition being faced, we can consider the difference between at least two basic types of fear, one seeming fear a help and one seeming fear a hindrance to survival.

Fear can be an important message from us to ourselves. *Can be.* When used well, fear serves a purpose. However, when used well, what we call "fear" is perhaps better described as *protective awareness*. For example, being afraid of an auto accident does less to prevent an accident than being very alert, highly aware of the other vehicles, people, animals, et cetera on the road.

Paying attention is a very good idea. Being so scared that you cannot protect yourself is not a good idea. When

ADVENTURES IN CHANGES, TRANSITIONS, AND DEATHS

fear clouds the mind, the attention, the consciousness, it is not being used well; it is perhaps even *blinding fear*.

Note: This distinction is especially critical on the population or societal level. First however, note that: Not everyone who warns of physical, environmental, political, economic, or other danger or disaster is sick with blinding fear. Some of these persons are calling important developments to our attention, suggesting that, in order to have a *conscious say in* or *conscious response to* the course of events, we pay attention and maybe even take action. Too often, those who seek to alert us to things, events, or forces which may affect us undesirably and against our will, are criticized or labeled as "paranoid" or "overly fearful" or "crazy." This is unfortunate, as protective awareness is of great value. A respectable scientist, analyst, futurist, or prophet is often taken far too lightly.

The problem is that we, our minds (or perhaps better stated, our brains) have a difficult time knowing what to

believe, how to tell the difference between useful information coming out of protective awareness and the static and chaos that comes from the projection of blinding fear. We humans have lived with so many fear-inducing lies for so long that we confuse these with valid warnings of impending danger. It becomes frighteningly difficult to tell the difference.

Furthermore, the brain's blinding fear responses are far more rapid, almost instantaneous, when compared to the brain's protective awareness thoughts. Rapid instinct-based brain responses (such as the fight-flight-freeze response we may exhibit in emergencies) are indeed set into motion far more rapidly than slower more cognitive-processing-like brain functions. For example, the brain can trigger an automatic instinctive response to a perceived threat in some five hundred (or fewer) milliseconds, in about half a second or less. However, for the brain to think through and weigh the meaning of a perceived physical threat, can take several seconds or even minutes – and quite

ADVENTURES IN CHANGES, TRANSITIONS, AND DEATHS

frankly even hours or days. (Indeed, the matter of the possible threat of climate change appears to be taking many human minds many years, even decades, perhaps centuries, to consider.)

DEFINING THE APOCALYPSE SYNDROME

Why are we unable to clearly sense this difference between protective awareness and blinding fear? It appears we frequently do not realize there is a difference. (As noted above, different brain functions operating at different speeds, are considering these two seeming fears, the protective awareness and the blinding fear.) And yet, knowing the difference between protective awareness and blinding fear can be essential to survival.

The tendency to think in terms of danger, disaster, calamity itself does not itself protect us. While the possibility of calamity may be truly frightening, an extreme almost single-minded, even blinding focus on the possibility of calamity itself can distract us from what we may be able to do to address this possibility.

Somehow, given our tendency to focus on the images and ideas that shock our brain into focusing on them, we are wired to address what calls our attention most. Where images of calamity draw our attention, these may produce in our brain and mind that rapid blinding fear response noted above, rather than a thought through protective awareness function. This book defines this blinding fear tendency as a syndrome, a syndrome we are wired to experience, what this book defines as being:

The Apocalypse Syndrome.

We have been biologically and socially wired, both genetically and culturally programmed, to carry within us this condition, this disease I am defining here, this *apocalypse syndrome*.

ADVENTURES IN CHANGES, TRANSITIONS, AND DEATHS

Take some time to think about the meaning of apocalypse and what your conscious mind does with this concept. Whether or not your subconscious mind pays any attention to this concept is less important for the moment. And, your subconscious mind may not be easy to hear.

APOKALYPSIS

The term "*apocalypse*" comes from the Greek word "*apokalypsis*" or "disclosure." Apocalypse is said to be some kind of major all-involving disaster in which forces of good and evil clash, and in which, in the end, only so-called supernatural intervention can preserve good.

According to most definitions of apocalypse, communication with divine forces should reveal (or predict) the timing, the force, and the characteristics of an apocalypse. Many religions therefore include "divine revelation." Some of these revelations are said to come to all

humans directly from God; however, apparently, in said reality, only a few humans can read these.

Many revelations are said to come from God but through designated human go-betweens or intermediaries who may be shamans, religious leaders, or persons with special abilities or special statuses.

Most religions and even mythologies include references to one or more apocalypses or cataclysms. These are generally said to take place at the end of a cycle of time: It is said that, at the end of such a cycle, piety will be dead; fire, drought and famine will ravage the Earth; and then a century or a long spell of death will follow. Despite flooding, all the moisture on and in the Earth will begin to dry up. Eventually, a universal conflagration of some sort will eliminate the last of the human occupants and all the Earth will be consumed in a vast whirlpool of flame. There is usually a supernatural way for "believers" and "the chosen ones" to survive.

ADVENTURES IN CHANGES, TRANSITIONS, AND DEATHS

This is standard apocalypse teaching. Depictions of this process do appear again and again in human religion and mythology. Many of these myths include the same ingredients -- increasing tribulation, the moral dissolution of human kind; the emergence of some kind of major war; the fracturing and collapse of the Earth's crust; and, later, the sinking of land masses, even entire continents, into the sea; the atmosphere becoming darkened; stars (including comets and meteors and maybe even moons) crashing down to Earth from the sky; and a massive fire of some sort filling much of the atmosphere.

Of course, this end is also viewed as a beginning, as new yugas or time cycles begin after major apocalypses, with the same cycles then repeatedly appearing. Eventually, the same ultimate fate evolves. Again and again, from the spoils, from the ashes of the cosmic fire, arises the phoenix, the flight of life, born anew.

PRIMER FOR LIFE'S MINOR AND MAJOR CHALLENGES AND PASSAGES

This quick overview is not to minimize the reality of apocalypse. Modern science tells us that the Earth has surely witnessed comet impacts and massive disasters of global proportions which killed off entire groups of species -- dinosaurs, for example.

There is more to history on Earth than we teach ourselves. Much of the truth about Earth's history has been lost. However, the collective memory has managed to keep some form of this information alive for us, preserving it not only in mythical and religious form throughout history, but also in symbolic imagery ...

deeply imbedded in our collective memory or mind --
perhaps even encoded into the genetics
which grow our brain and mind.

Here, we must pause to wonder whether, if images of apocalypse are indeed coded into our collective memories, how did those images get there -- and are they placed there to protect us, or to scare us into being more easily controlled?

ADVENTURES IN CHANGES, TRANSITIONS, AND DEATHS

PERSONAL APOCALYPSE

Whatever its means of and motive for coming to us may be, information about the possibility of global or massive disaster is useful. Mankind desires this knowledge. Humanity instinctively keeps its sensors out -- maintains a protective awareness regarding past and potential global cataclysms. (Refer to other books in this KEYS TO CONSCIOUSNESS AND SURVIVAL SERIES, such as the OVERRIDING THE EXTINCTION SCENARIO books, listed in the Recommended Reading List found in the APPENDICES Section of this present book.)

Of course, both species-wide and individual, personal, awareness of possible or impending danger is essential. Fortunately, this awareness is built into instinctual, even automatic, responses we are wired to have such as the flight, fight, and freeze response. The problem is that, with this healthy instinct can come a deeply buried blindness, even the blinding fear referred to earlier in this chapter.

Even if various people do not feel themselves to be fearful, they cannot help but be affected by imagery buried deeply within the collective mind. And, it is these traditionally and genetically preserved visions that at times can bring on an unspoken free-floating fear, even the great Fear of Death.

This discussion is important in that it traces the source of our individual awareness of possible disaster back through human history and Earth history to pictures of actual disaster which have indeed taken place and can indeed happen again. (See the in-depth discussions of historical and global trauma in other books in this and related series by this author. Refer to Recommended Reading in the APPENDICES section of this present book.)

Every living thing has deeply ingrained survival mechanisms which should promote an ongoing protective

ADVENTURES IN CHANGES, TRANSITIONS, AND DEATHS

awareness in each of us. However, we somehow translate this high and pure awareness down into a lower emotional state which clouds the intelligently protective personal consciousness.

HOW THE APOCALYPSE SYNDROME BECOMES PERSONAL

Many people bring awareness and acceptance of the reality of global, solar, galactic, even cosmic, danger and cataclysm down to the personal level. As a result of this instinctive translation, some may start seeing potential apocalypse everywhere. Protective awareness and blinding fear are then mingled. Perceptions are then clouded and very subjective.

This is how personal apocalypses, real or imagined, can be tailor-made for us, by our subjective perceptions of our experiences, and of the information we have regarding possible upcoming experiences. Indeed, these personalized

apocalypses can include and confuse real and imagined, past and present, global and local, population and personal, minor and major, traumatic life experiences.

And, to further cloud the issue, as problematic as this confusion is, it contains within it some degree of honesty: A child crying in pain on the other side of the planet may in some way be heard or felt by an intuitive or in some way hyper-sensitive person standing here. On some level, all of us are always in touch with the sensations being experienced by members of our own species, wherever they are, and even by other life forms everywhere. (Note: Some nursing mothers have discovered this sensitivity when their babies cause them to drip milk by crying, even out of earshot, across town!) We may all be this sensitive, whether or not we recognize this. This is a basic survival mechanism -- sensitivity to the needs of the species.

Personal apocalypse consciousness is a reality, whether or not a person is conscious of having this consciousness. Population, even species, pain IS personal

ADVENTURES IN CHANGES, TRANSITIONS, AND DEATHS

suffering -- even when this translation is entirely subconscious.

HOWEVER, THERE CAN BE A POSITIVE APOCALYPSE CONSCIOUSNESS

Apocalypse awareness is with us. It would be dishonest to say that intense experiences, challenging transitions, events which may be perceived as terrible, will never take place. But it is also dishonest to say that there is no positive or at least constructive way of seeing these.

Let's call this *positive apocalypse consciousness*, and say this is essential. This constructive view (and use of our instinctive apocalypse awareness) will purify the application of protective awareness and reduce its being mingled with blinding fear. Positive apocalypse consciousness is a state of knowing how to admit to oneself the difference between blinding fear and protective awareness -- and how to resist labeling one's sensations as

one or the other of these fears when others label these for you.

Positive apocalypse consciousness also involves a sense of rising to meet the challenge of any transition, of any death. Seeing a purpose, a positive outcome, as a distinct possibility -- even if that positive outcome is simply that one's SELF, one's consciousness, CAN (in some form) make it through an ordeal -- is essential. *Adventures in Changes, Transitions, and Deaths* herewith covers the basics of this positive consciousness.

Allow the ideas offered on these pages to dialogue with your heart, mind, soul, with your own personal consciousness. Question as much of this as you feel driven to. Honest questioning and ongoing dialogue can be a means of discovering truth for yourself. And, this can be the surest route to knowing more about our options in life, also in seeming end-of-life, and perhaps even in so-called after-life circumstances.

ADVENTURES IN CHANGES, TRANSITIONS, AND DEATHS

3
Physical Death As A Model

This chapter looks at physical (biological) death, its processes, and some of its characteristics, to provide a basis for the overall discussion of change, transition, and death this book addresses.

In seeing death as a process, we can become ever more aware of what death itself is about. Seeing death as a process of moving beyond biological, emotional, and mental patterns is key in understanding the change, transition, and death process itself -- whether it be the in-life death of a behavioral pattern, or of a phase of life, or even an end-of-life death.

No discussion of death can go on without some review of the phases of physical death. This is not only because physical death is what is most commonly thought of when the word "death" is used. This is also because physical death is a fantastic metaphor for many other endings, crises of change, and transitions. After all:

physical (biological) death

appears to have a beginning and an ending

AND

- o appears to have stages along the way;
- o is a process rather than a single momentary event;
- o offers the opportunity to more or less consciously navigate the process;
- o includes options and choices, although these are more available to us once we understand what these are;
- o and, may even involve several forms of SELF that may either continue to live, or choose to die along the way.

The entire notion of surviving death (and transition) becomes more clear when we think in terms of the possibility that: we have not only a physical biological body that may die, but also an emotional body, and then even a mental body that may choose to live on.

ADVENTURES IN CHANGES, TRANSITIONS, AND DEATHS

You will see the value of this comparison between physical and other forms of transition and death as you read on. Try not to allow a fear of death or the sense that "this has nothing to do with my life right now" to stop you from really reading this chapter. If you step back and look, you may find that your transition processes, especially the more difficult ones, are unusually parallel to physical death processes.

IN THE PROCESS OF DYING:
THE FIRST DEATH

Each and every physical death is different; however, there are general events and other similarities among them. Some of the variation in the dying process relates to the style of death one undergoes or perhaps even chooses, (if one has the opportunity to choose, that is).

In this brief discussion of the process of biologically dying, many details are not included. Readers are encouraged to learn these details in depth, elsewhere. Here,

the focus is on: how the SELF experiences dying; what the SELF may want to know before experiencing dying; and, by implication -- how physical biological death processes can parallel other in-life transition processes, and vice versa.

The Concept Of Conscious Dying

An opening note here. We can consider even the meaning of consciousness itself as we talk about change, transition, and death processes. The idea that we want to be as aware, as conscious as we can, as we move through our lives is not surprising. However, there is always room to become ever more aware, to participate in our own processes ever more consciously.

Even when it comes to biological death itself, the matter of consciousness is highly relevant. In terms of this book's expanded view of the consciousness, we can say that conscious dying may take place whether or not a person is medically defined as being in a state of consciousness.

ADVENTURES IN CHANGES, TRANSITIONS, AND DEATHS

Learning what it means to be ever more aware, ever more conscious, while living daily life, can be preparation for maintaining consciousness later. The idea that conscious dying can be key in survival may have profound implications.

(For more discussion of this matter, see other books in this KEYS TO CONSCIOUSNESS AND SURVIVAL SERIES, such as Volume 7, KEYS TO ACCESSING THE BEYOND, and Volume 14, HOW TO DIE AND SURVIVE, BOOK THREE.)

An Early Phase Of Physical Dying

Quite often, although not always, even an early phase of physical dying may be experienced semi-consciously. Note that even when not appearing to be at all conscious, the dying person may nevertheless be more conscious than he or she may appear.

The Brain Early In The Dying Process

Usually, early in the dying process, blood pressure substantially reduces. The brain therefore finds itself running short of its normal supply of oxygen and sugar. So the brain turns on a compensatory mechanism which dilates its blood vessels and draws extra blood from wherever it might be stored in the body. What this does is give the sugar-hungry brain a brief increase in its blood sugar. The brain hangs on to its biologically-fueled inner consciousness this way.

Moving Into A Next Phase Of Physical Dying

At this point, the brain is, for a brief time, receiving a much enriched supply of food. With this increase in brain food, the dying person is able to flashback or even to rapidly review his or her entire life. In a sense, consciousness is actually intensified here, although little emotion is felt in these flashback moments. This is because this intense

ADVENTURES IN CHANGES, TRANSITIONS, AND DEATHS

review is a higher cognitive activity, with little if any involvement of lower emotional processes.

At this time, the brain, mainly the cortex, is working at a feverous pitch. Now, the brain is consuming sugar faster than it can get it. This results in the brain's sensing that it cannot continue to fuel the intense flashback process.

When this awareness is registered, the brain begins moving into the second phase of physical dying. The brain is operating at a very high frequency now, maintaining what are called rapid rhythmical beta waves with some spurts of alpha. This generates what some people who practice meditation can bring about for themselves without dying -- a sense of bliss, a transcendent sense.

Moving Deeper Into The Dying Process

Whether or not appearing to be conscious in medical terms, the brain is quite conscious of this state of euphoria or intense happiness. Yet, this is not really an emotional

experience in the way we experience joy in daily life. This is a very special, very high, state of emotional bliss.

Now physical dying is not complete but is drawing to a close. Up to this time, medical or other efforts to revive the dying person, to return the dying person to the biological body, may still be successful. Yet, many a dying individual, persuaded by the profound euphoria, is committed to dying by now. Now many a dying person wants to die this death.

Remember, if and when you find yourself in this state, you do have a right to move on. At this point in your dying, it is going to be important to remember that many times you can still easily make a conscious decision to either go ahead and die, or to come back into your body. I say conscious here, although this conscious decision may be made whether or not you are medically conscious by outside definitions. (See other books in this series where the matter of the SELF as the consciousness surviving is discussed in great depth – such as the HOW TO DIE AND SURVIVE

ADVENTURES IN CHANGES, TRANSITIONS, AND DEATHS

books. Refer again to Recommended Reading listed in the APPENDICES section of this present book.)

You may actually be able to make this decision to survive in some form without medical intervention pushing you in either direction. You are actually quite powerful at this juncture. You just need to know this at this time.

The Moving On Phase

If the dying person is moving on into death, actual physical dying begins here. Now the body will stop breathing, the physical eyes will stop seeing, although they have most likely stopped looking before this time. The brain will stop running, being out of sugar.

The dying individual is quite aware of these sensations, however in a detached way. There is no suffering in this. The last words, if any, will have been uttered -- usually mumbled or whispered -- by now. There is no suffering in this.

There will be no further physical sensation unless the dying individual imagines there to be. This is tricky because the imagination cannot arise from the brain at this point. Most persons who are able to be conscious during this time will feel that they are not in their bodies.

Remember that this is a good time to observe how much of your sensation of your reality – and of your actual SELF -- you may be able to conduct with your non-physical mind or consciousness, whether or not you have a functioning biological body or working sensory organs.

Continued Awareness Of The SELF

Now there is, or can be, a continued awareness of self, and a looking back at (or down at) at the biological body which is being shed. Some beings see someone kissing their bodies goodbye and momentarily experience a vague detached sense of wanting a physical body again. Others are immediately relieved to let go.

ADVENTURES IN CHANGES, TRANSITIONS, AND DEATHS

Stay Conscious Here

Stay conscious here. Remind yourself that you can stay conscious here. You will remember these words on this page if you wish to. We have not been told we can stay conscious through our processes. Sometimes even just knowing this allows us to know this later, when we need to know this to survive.

So do stay conscious here, whether or not you appear to be conscious to doctors or to other onlookers. Many of those around you may know, or at least sense, that on some level you are still alive as a conscious being.

Notice when your "mind" is seeing, feeling, "thinking." Notice your location in what you have been calling space and time. Notice your emotional detachment, or better stated, that you have detached from your emotions.

Letting Go: Freeing The Soul

Letting go is critical here. You should remember that you can stay conscious as you do so. It is important to understand the letting go or severance process. Physical death is the withdrawal of the SELF, or the spirit, or what some may call the soul, from what may be its two anchors: the heart and the pineal gland in the brain. This withdrawal from the heart and from the head is said to cut off the two cords or streams of energy which unite the ethereal soul with the physical body -- the blood stream and the endocrine stream or system.

This cutting off is said to cut the tie, the connection between body and soul. Sometimes a body resists the departure of the spirit or soul which has inhabited it, and then this severance process is slower.

Stay conscious here. It might be better said that some souls, not understanding this process, do not fully cut these cords, these streams between the dimensions. If you stay

ADVENTURES IN CHANGES, TRANSITIONS, AND DEATHS

quite conscious here, you can cut these cords, these umbilical cords, for yourself and deliver yourself into a new dimension of your personal consciousness, of your own reality.

IN THE PROCESS OF DYING:
THE SECOND DEATH

Now you are finished with physical death. Once you pass out of the biological body or physical vehicle, you have passed from the first episode of death or the first death, which is physical, on to the second death, which is not physical. In this next death comes what has been called the "astral death" – here let's say this is the death of the emotional body.

> And, you have formed
> quite a complex emotional body
> during this lifetime!

Once the physical house of the body is empty, it begins to decompose.[2] You may want to think that death is complete at the physical end, after the phases of physical death described above. Yet, the next dying, that astral or emotional body death, is as much a great passage, if not more. The individual who has just lost her or his biological body may still retain many of the feelings and awareness-es of others' feelings acquired while in that body.

Moving On Toward Non-Physicality

A highly trained being can leave the physical vehicle quite consciously and, in full waking awareness, preserve the continuity of consciousness while moving from the physical plane-based biological body to what feels to be the non-physical after-death state:

from physicality to non-physicality.

---

[2] Note that following even medically declared (biological) death, many of the body's cells live on, with some cells reverting to a sort of stem cell state, or what some may see as similar to fetal cell state.

ADVENTURES IN CHANGES, TRANSITIONS, AND DEATHS

You can do this, you can generate this awareness and possibility in your mind, in your consciousness. You can do this, whether or not you have received intensive training, especially if you can stay somewhat aware, conscious -- and remember that all your feelings are part of an emotional body that you are shedding. If you stay stuck, trapped in your emotional body, your consciousness, your energy and power, may weaken.

Those who do not understand this second stage of death -- emotional death – may enter it anxiously, perhaps still experiencing what feels to be fear, or anger, and or confusion, and needlessly waste their spiritual or personal energy (however this energy will be interpreted and experienced at this time). (Having these sensations at this juncture in the dying process may feel to be odd, as there is no physical biological body to form these emotions.)

Try to take this information in by studying it from time to time. You will remember bits of this description

many times during your livings and dyings. You may want to read more intricate reviews of the biological dying process than we have space for here.

IN THE PROCESS OF DYING:
THE THIRD DEATH

Eventually, whatever her or his awareness, the physically dead individual can and likely must leave behind all emotional connection to the physical plane and move on. This letting go is a critical and very difficult process for many. At this point, the mind or the SELF, however the SELF is experienced at this point, senses that what <u>may</u> come next is the dissipation of the mental energy assumed during the recent incarnation -- which lingers after the emotional energy has been shed. This is the third death.

It is said that very few spirits are "evolved enough" to succeed in fully completing this third death and, in so doing, crossing the threshold beyond the death cycle. It is also said that most fail at this death and therefore must

ADVENTURES IN CHANGES, TRANSITIONS, AND DEATHS

recycle again and again until some day they will finally succeed.

Be alert here and question this particular message. This message is not necessarily wrong. However, the surrendering of one's mental energy must be studied closely, as you may choose not to die this final mental body death, *in essence, not to die.* And, you do have a right to choose not to die. (See other books in this KEYS TO CONSCIOUSNESS AND SURVIVAL SERIES, where this matter is defined and discussed in detail, such as Volume 6, OVERRIDING THE EXTINCTION SCENARIO, PART TWO.)

Think about this mental death. Ask: if you do go ahead and die this third and final phase, where does your SELF, your mental energy go? Where do you go? Do you want to go there? Do you understand that you may be able to survive biological death if you do not undergo mental body death, that this is your right to learn about, practice,

and then decide for yourself? (Again, see other books in this series for definitions and details on this matter, such as Volume 14, HOW TO DIE AND SURVIVE, BOOK THREE.)

Are you willing to stay conscious right on through the very challenging death process in order to look closely at where you are sending your precious human energy at this juncture? Consider the possibility that you can retain the option of surviving your biological and emotional deaths as your own personal mental body, your own personal consciousness. (Again, for details on this matter, see Volume 14, HOW TO DIE AND SURVIVE, BOOK THREE.)

You Can Be Navigating Your Death Process

You can consciously navigate your death in order to consciously avoid surrendering your mental energy -- energy you cultivated during your physical lifetime -- to a force that may use it for other than you would freely choose to have it used.

ADVENTURES IN CHANGES, TRANSITIONS, AND DEATHS

Accept responsibility for this awareness. You may be able to free yourself as well as others from being cycled (against your and their wills) through the human energy plantation and other farms and factories such as this one that may exist throughout the cosmos. We will return to this profound matter later (and in other books in this KEYS TO CONSCIOUSNESS AND SURVIVAL SERIES. See Reading List in the APPENDICES section of this present book). Whatever <u>conscious focus</u> on moving through the physical (or actual) and emotional (or astral) episodes of death is achieved by the dying individual will serve as great training.

The intelligent, survival-oriented, road map from physical (biological) body death, to emotional body death, to optional mental body death – which is the death of the personal consciousness, of the SELF, is one drawn by repeated exploration of the process. Consciously navigating (and even surviving) the three deaths, each as a conscious process, may be the greatest challenge for a being. Yet, once we know we have this option, survival is itself the option.

ABOUT THE METAPHOR

And here is the metaphor: ***Navigating*** one's death is a process. There is an art and a science AND A POLITIC of dying that we can learn -- and that we can apply to all types of transitions, whether these be in daily physical plane life, or in so-called end of life, or even in after life.

A QUESTION OF RIGHTS

Your right to die in the manner you choose for yourself must be exercised while you are on Earth and in your physical biological body, as well as in the time after you leave your biological body. Human rights can extend far beyond the physical plane.

ADVENTURES IN CHANGES, TRANSITIONS, AND DEATHS

NOTE ON THE FOLLOWING DIAGRAMS

The following diagrams offer visualizations of: the relationships between the unconscious self, and degrees of consciousness (Figure 3.1.); the notion of the several bodies we carry, ranging from physical body to other levels of non-physicality where we may also live (Figure 3.2.); the coordination of biological and other body level deaths (Figure 3.3.); and, descriptions of the three deaths (Figure 3.4.)

PRIMER FOR LIFE'S MINOR AND MAJOR CHALLENGES AND PASSAGES

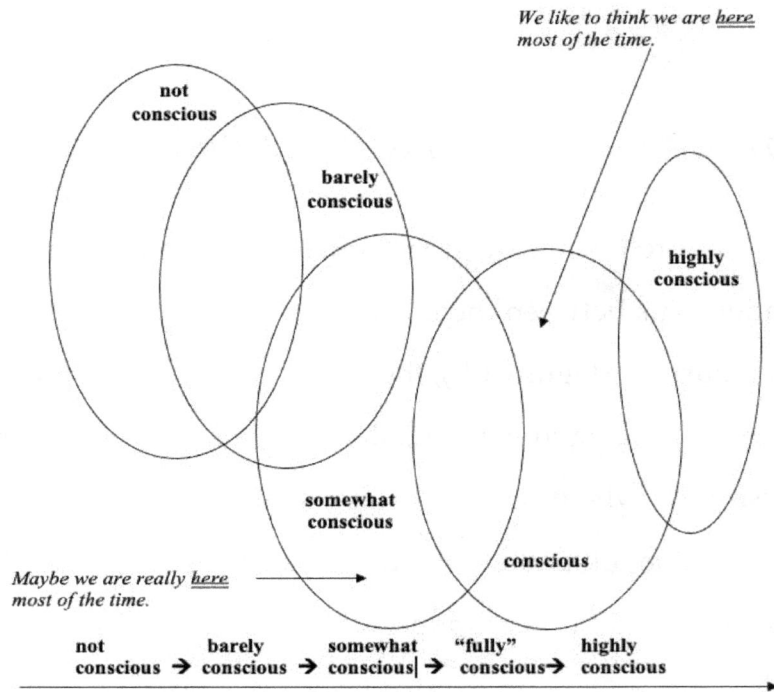

degree of consciousness

**FIGURE 3.1.
OVERLAPPING LEVELS OF PERCEIVED CONSCIOUSNESS**

Where are we in daily "waking" life?
Where do we think we are in daily "waking" life?
Where do we appear to others to be in daily "waking" life?
Where do we appear to others to be when in various phases of physical death?
Where do we appear to ourselves to be when in various phases of physical death?

ADVENTURES IN CHANGES, TRANSITIONS, AND DEATHS

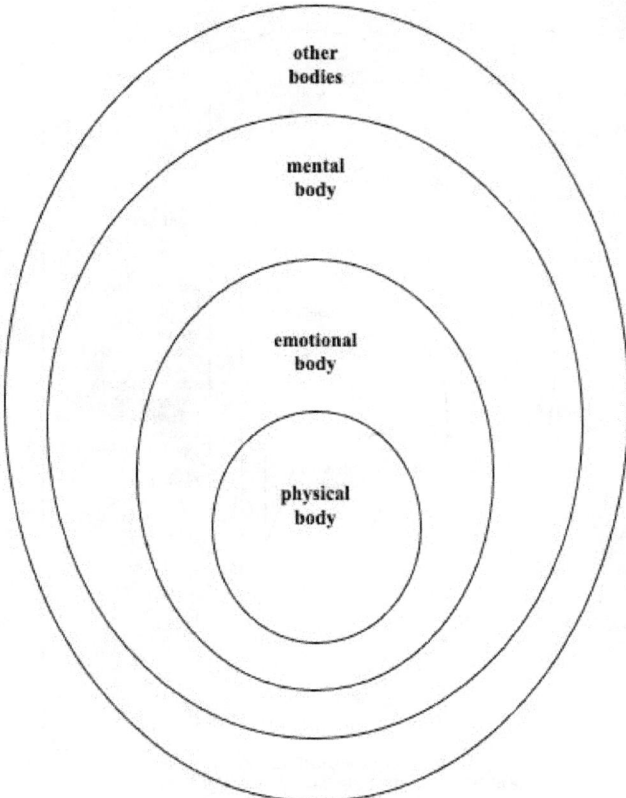

**FIGURE 3.2.
OUR MANY BODIES**

We are so much more than meets the eye.
Who we are and where we are is something the physical eye may not tell us.
What dies when the physical body dies?
What does not have to die?

PRIMER FOR LIFE'S MINOR AND MAJOR CHALLENGES AND PASSAGES

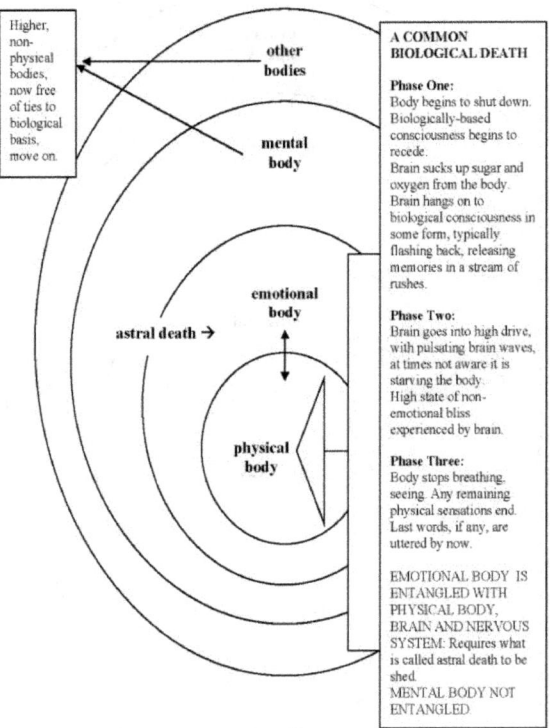

FIGURE 3.3.
COORDINATING BIOLOGICAL AND OTHER-BASED DEATH
Physical (biological) death involves the stages of the separation of the life of the being from the physical body, with one common pattern of physical death proceeding as in the three phases of biological death listed above.
Non-biological death or transition typically involves departing the physical body, and the emotional body, and moving into the bodies which are not biologically based. These non-biologically-based bodies may be retained or shed.

ADVENTURES IN CHANGES, TRANSITIONS, AND DEATHS

PHYSICAL/BIOLOGICAL BODY DEATH

Physical/biological death involves the stages of the separation of the life of the being from the physical body, with a common pattern of physical death proceeding as in the three phases of biological death listed below:

Phase One: Biological Body Death
Body begins to shut down.
Biologically based consciousness begins to recede.
Brain sucks up sugar and oxygen from the body.
Brain hangs on to biological consciousness in some form,
typically flashing back,
releasing memories in a stream of rushes.

Phase Two: Biological Body Death
Brain goes into high drive, with pulsating brain waves, starving the body.
High state of non-emotional bliss experienced by brain.

Phase Three: Biological Body Death
Body stops breathing, seeing. Any remaining physical sensations end.
Last words, if any, have been uttered by now.

EMOTIONAL BODY DEATH
Emotional body is entangled with physical body, brain, and nervous system:
Requires "astral" or other death to be shed.
Mental body not entangled.

MENTAL BODY NEED NOT DIE
Non-biological death can include the mental body. However, the mental body can free itself from ties to biological death to **survive transition**. Transition typically involves departing the physical body, and the emotional body, and moving into bodies (if any)
which are not biologically-based.

These non-biologically-based bodies
and their patterns may be retained or shed,
MAY BE CONSCIOUSLY RETAINED OR SHED.

****

Figure 3.4.
THE THREE DEATHS

PRIMER FOR LIFE'S MINOR AND MAJOR CHALLENGES AND PASSAGES

ADVENTURES IN CHANGES, TRANSITIONS, AND DEATHS

4
Allowing One's Patterning To Die

All changes, transitions, and deaths involve the shedding of patterns. Awareness of patterning, and then of pattern shedding itself as a concept, is central in this book's discussion of death and dying ideas.

Patterns can be quite useful, even essential. Patterns can help us, and they can hold us on track. Yet, problem patterns can control us, entangle us, harm us, weigh us down. In essence, patterns, including problem patterns, can resist dying. <u>*It is then that the death of the problem pattern is the freeing of us.*</u>

Understanding the nature of patterning, of the webs we weave as we live, and of how difficult it can be to free ourselves of patterns, to let patterns die, can be key in understanding death processes -- whether these be pattern deaths promoting recovery, healing, or other forms of change and transition, or physical death of the biological body itself.

We often describe ourselves and each other as "creatures of habit." Think about what this means. This

means we may be somewhat like robots -- nice, soft cuddly ones maybe, but nevertheless, programmable bio-machines.

This chapter is included here to explain that a healthy transition -- even the death of a particular problem behavioral pattern within a life -- requires recognizing patterns that must be amended or shed. This death of a behavior is about modifying or blocking or eliminating undesirable patterning, programming – *about letting patterns go in order to move through our changes, transitions, and deaths as consciously as we can.*

OUR RIGID ADDICTIONS
TO LIFE AS WE KNOW IT

There is more to our resistance to death than the blinding fear of the known or unknown, and on the other hand, the protective awareness, both discussed in Chapter 2. There is a programing wired into us, into our brains, that causes us to hold on to our patterns, whether these are healthy patterns or unhealthy patterns, to allow these patterns themselves to survive.

ADVENTURES IN CHANGES, TRANSITIONS, AND DEATHS

(The matter of patterns themselves seeking to survive, being designed to survive, is explained in depth in the book, SEEING THE HIDDEN FACE OF ADDICTION: DETECTING AND CONFRONTING THIS INVASIVE PRESENCE. See reading list in the APPENDICES Section at the end of this present book.)

There is a deep, genetically-ordained drive within every genetically coded living organism to become addicted to patterns. And this is, for the most part, a survival-oriented tendency. After all, it is essential that we form behavioral as well as biological patterns in order to live in our biological body here in the physical plane.

It is essential we can respond automatically and rapidly, without taking the time to think, in what may be urgent or even life-threatening situations. Otherwise, how many people could automatically leap out of the way of a falling boulder in the instant needed to survive?

It is also convenient that certain necessary behaviors become habitual. How many people could stop their car at a red light on time if they had to take the time to figure out what the red light signified and how to stop the car? It is good that we are programmed to learn to do some things automatically. But there is a down-side to this automatic programming capability of ours.

We have begun to recognize the down side. In recent times, humans have become increasingly conscious of the problem of addiction to destructive and dangerous behavioral patterns, such as patterns of compulsive overeating, drug and alcohol addiction, sex addiction, and workaholism.

These are explicit additions -- more obvious, visible addictions. These behaviors tend to be more easily recognized than do other more hidden, more implicit addictions.

ADVENTURES IN CHANGES, TRANSITIONS, AND DEATHS

EXPLICIT PATTERN ADDICTIONS ARE SYMPTOMS

Yet, explicit addictions are, basically, only symptoms of implicit addictions to deeper behavioral, emotional, and energetic patterns. And, implicit pattern addiction, even when life threatening, does not always signal its presence through explicit addictions. Implicit pattern addiction can be very difficult to detect.

Pattern addiction is part of the human condition. Pattern addiction comes with the genetic package, which is supposedly and usually survival-oriented. So, should we concern ourselves with our hidden pattern addictions? Yes!

This is the message here: The more prepared we are to detect and transcend *detrimental* physical, emotional, social, and cognitive behavior patterns -- even and especially the hidden ones -- when these are indeed problematic patterns -- to let them change or die, the more active a role we can play in our emotional, physical, and spiritual health. And, the more free will we can have both here and BEYOND (whatever this BEYOND means to each of us).

Most implicit pattern addictions, even those behind problem patterns, are built over a long period of time. This is because most neurological programming -- which involves the establishment of electrical or energetic patterns throughout the brain and body -- takes place over time.

Such patterning becomes detrimental when harmful to the emotional, physical, and or spiritual well-being of the individual (and or family or community or society or globe). Problem pattern addiction frequently manifests itself in explicit symptoms such as the destructive addictions named above, and may also relate to some physical pain, some chronic ailments, and possibly even some diseases.

Some pattern addiction is so subtle, so very implicit, that it involves holding patterns or blockages of necessary electrical charges, and of full blood flow, and of ample

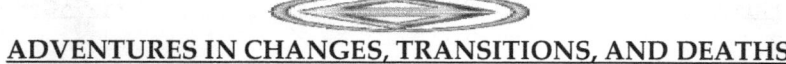
ADVENTURES IN CHANGES, TRANSITIONS, AND DEATHS

oxygen to remote parts of the body. By *remote*, I mean nerve endings, organs, brain cells, and other tissues of which we are often unaware. Remote then, does not signify physical distance here, it signifies distance from aware consciousness. The more aware one is of something, the closer one is to it.

For example, tight musculature surrounding digestive organs can interfere with the transmission of oxygen and neurological impulses involved in building or using digestive enzymes. Tight musculature in the head and neck can lead to jaw grinding. As Oriental medicine suggests, most afflictions are the product of energy flow disturbances.

A rebalancing or correction of troubled patterns in the transmission of neurological energy and electrical charges moving or not moving throughout the body may alleviate or at least soothe many health problems. When this rebalancing (which is often difficult to achieve for oneself

until the process is learned) occurs, a harmful energetic pattern, *the implicit pattern of the affliction* – perhaps pattern of physical pain, or drug use, or troubled state of mind, or problem emotional cycle-- is then broken.

Without correcting the underlying and more implicit psycho-biological pattern addictions, the built-in addiction patternings, without amending or erasing the programming *behind* the physical and psychological symptoms, the same or similar symptoms can continue, recur, and expand. This is, of course, due in part to the understandable limitations current medical and psychological technologies face in treating surface addictions and surface symptoms in the addressing of extremely deep programming to be patterned.

DRUG ADDICTION AS AN EXAMPLE

Drug addiction offers one of the most tangible examples of patterning and some of the most tangible evidence that addiction to a pattern can be transcended.

ADVENTURES IN CHANGES, TRANSITIONS, AND DEATHS

Drug addiction (we must include alcohol whenever we refer to drugs here) is therefore the primary, but not only, example in this book. You will see the parallels between drug addiction and all pattern addiction.

Let's examine the societal implications of this threatening explicit addiction so common in modern times. Many illusions surround drug (including alcohol) addiction. One is the illusion of health. Far too many addicted individuals are in a state of denial about their health problems. Too many claim that they are not addicted and use their seemingly good health as proof that they are not addicted. But their lives are wounded.

These people are operating under the *illusion* of health as well as under the *illusion* of not being addicted. Most people who suffer from any form of problem pattern addiction are in a state of denial about its actual severity, if they admit its existence at all. This denial is often part of the programming by the problem pattern to let the pattern

survive, even it if kills it host. (See again the book where this issue is explained in depth, SEEING THE HIDDEN FACE OF ADDICTION: DETECTING AND CONFRONTING THIS INVASIVE PRESENCE. See Reading List in the APPENDICES section of this present book.)

IN THIS CRISIS IS OPPORTUNITY

Yet, in this crisis of the mind, heart, soul, and will, lies the possibility of transformation, and of transcendence. (*Transformation* and *transcendence* are not typical listings in medical school curricula.) Crisis is opportunity, opportunity for attention.

Most people wait for a major psychological or physical crisis to begin to even vaguely address their pattern addictions. For drug addicted persons, this crisis has sometimes been called *hitting bottom*. Hitting bottom can compel addicted or otherwise afflicted individuals to seize the opportunity to learn, and to care, about their mental,

ADVENTURES IN CHANGES, TRANSITIONS, AND DEATHS

physical, and spiritual health. Hitting bottom is a call to action.

Many people who think that they have never been detrimentally pattern addicted may have not experienced this opportunity. Because the process of overcoming deep pattern addiction requires change on many levels, problem addiction can actually provide a rare opportunity for profound personal change, and for the realization of one's psychological, creative, and spiritual potentials.

HOW PATTERN ADDICTIONS CONTROL US

When a society, a globe full of societies, grows alarmed about drug trafficking, smuggling across borders, narcoterrorism, and drug addiction (as does ours from time to time), it is responding to explicit problems. And yet, there is an unspoken, intuitive understanding of the implicit ramifications of such explicit problems. Something about the deepest level of the human condition is being expressed.

The problem of addiction goes much deeper than a simple lack of knowledge as to "criminals'" whereabouts or a failure of border closure. Chemical dependence is only one expression of a far more common and more harmful behavior that afflicts our society: <u>destructive dependence patterning</u>. Anyone can fall into a destructive habit. Some people have a destructive dependence on food, others on sex, still others on the people in their close personal relationships -- some people have a destructive chemical dependence or another explicit addiction pattern.

The reality of human existence is that a "little addict person" lurks within all of us, as we are wired to addict ourselves to patterns. To better understand this little addict person we all share, let's consider two key concepts: *addictive materialism* and *addictive inadequacy*. These are most readily understood in cases of tangible addiction, because tangible explicit addiction patterns are more easily traced than more subtle explicit patterns, which may or may not have direct overt physical expression.

ADVENTURES IN CHANGES, TRANSITIONS, AND DEATHS

THESE ADDICTIONS APPLY TO ALL OF US

The problems of what I have come to call *addictive materialism* (dependence on outer means for solving inner problems) -- and of what I have come to define as *addictive inadequacy* (an inadequate internal coping mechanism) are common to a greater portion of society than the mere population of those addicted to chemicals such as drugs and alcohol. How many of us go shopping and end up overspending when we are bored, depressed, or faced with a crisis? How many of us have trouble dealing with the realities of life and are forced to depend on externalities?

Not all of us are addicted to dangerous chemicals. However, we all exhibit signs of both addictive materialism and addictive inadequacy. Each of us regularly seeks to compensate for these addictive characteristics within ourselves. This means that the addicted individual is not alone, and not unlike the seemingly non-addicted person. We all have a great deal in common. If we are honest with

ourselves, we will admit that we have seen the pattern addict. And he, or she, is us.

HOW WE FORM PATTERN ADDICTIONS

What you do here, in your physical dimension, has effects far beyond the reality you see and know. PATTERN ADDICTIONS, WHATEVER THEIR SYMPTOMS, TRAP ENERGY. Be careful how you use your energy, whether it is your physical, your emotional, your financial, or your spiritual energy, or other form of energy.

Pattern addictions sneak up on people. Take, for example, the development of a drug addiction, or a relationship addiction, or any other explicit addiction. These standard addictions do not begin explicitly. You may even be in one right now and not realize it because it is not yet an explicit addiction. For example, an addiction to a drug or a specific behavior usually begins with *casual behavior*.

ADVENTURES IN CHANGES, TRANSITIONS, AND DEATHS

Casual behavior is light, experimental, seemingly without deep consequences. The experimenter lives in a society that appears to allow at least some degree of freedom to experiment and explore. "Try this just once...then decide if you want to try it again." Or, "I dare you to try this. ... Bet you can't eat just one. ... Come on, show us what a man (or woman) you are." Experimenting is a part of growing up. But sadly, much casual behavior becomes *regular behavior*.

Casual Behavior ----------> Regular Behavior

At some point, some regular behaviors become a bit too regular. When it is a problem behavior, the regular behavior can then become a troubled behavior.

Regular Behavior---------->Troubled Behavior

People who are exhibiting *troubled behavior* continue to do so in the face of adverse effects to themselves (their health, their mind, their work), their families, their

businesses, their neighborhoods, their societies. It is easy to slip from regular behavior to troubled behavior because the early signs of troubled behavior are subtle and often go undetected.

Again, consider drug use as a blatant example. Someone who has a few drinks at a bar on the way home from work, is already driving "under the influence" -- however slight that influence may seem -- of alcohol. Of course, driving home may be entirely possible. The point is that many users who are in a state of troubled behavior do not consider the risks that their use is posing to themselves or to others. They are not even aware of how easily they can slip from troubled behavior into full blown *addicted behavior*.

Casual ---> Regular ---> Troubled ---> Addicted
Behaviors

Fortunately, not everyone who tries alcohol or other drugs, or overeating, or gambling for example, travels this

ADVENTURES IN CHANGES, TRANSITIONS, AND DEATHS

tragic path. Some of these persons, these *casual behav<u>ors</u>* try a behavior once or a few times, and then consider the experiment completed. But all too commonly, casual behaviors unwittingly slip into regular behaviors. People may confidently tell themselves, "It can't happen to me. I'm too much in control of my life to develop an addiction to anything. I'm just having a little fun."

In reality, we are deluding ourselves. Case history after case history demonstrates that casual behaviors, without training regarding how to avoid programming oneself, dramatically increases the probability of developing a fully addicted behavior. And any behavior conducted regularly increases the chances of its being programmed into you.

This is an explanation of the descent into detrimental (problem) pattern addiction. Any behavior can be expressed once or twice. But somehow, we are blind to the crossing of the boundaries between casual and regular, regular and

troubled, troubled and addicted. Why? Because we are biologically wired to go onto automatic, programmed to slip unaware into both healthy and unhealthy pattern addictions.

THE FREEING AND RIGHT USE OF OUR ENERGY

Is this genetic programming mere happenstance? Is it the misfiring of the survival-oriented function (originally designed to have us automatically respond to definite dangers, even to seemingly lesser events such as red lights and other safety signals)? Or, are we prisoners of a mechanism buried deeply within our coding -- a mechanism rendering us readily programmed and obedient creatures of habit?

It is this essential programming to form habits, patterns, that can interfere with our changing, transitioning, and dying processes. After all, even survival-oriented programming such as patterning can run awry.

ADVENTURES IN CHANGES, TRANSITIONS, AND DEATHS

Yes, each of us carries within us, embedded right into us, at least thousands if not millions of patterns and sub-patterns, most all that are designed to survive, even when at our own expense. Here is where we can benefit by bringing ever more conscious awareness to our processes of changes, transitions, and pattern deaths.

PRIMER FOR LIFE'S MINOR AND MAJOR CHALLENGES AND PASSAGES

ADVENTURES IN CHANGES, TRANSITIONS, AND DEATHS

5
Death And Transcendence

We are wired to develop patterns we then live by, hold on to as long as we can. These patterns are generally wired to persist, to hold us in their structures, their webs. This chapter talks about -- how we move beyond these patterns, whether in change, transition, or death processes – and says that how we move beyond these patterns will determine the results of our processes.

Ultimately, reaching beyond, moving out of patterns that may not be allowing us to successfully change, transition, or die, requires a LEAP in awareness, even a transcendence of the patterns we are seeking to change, transition, and or die out of.

We become *addicted to the very programming* we would shed in transition and death processes. Thus we may be resisting this shedding. When this shedding -- this death of a pattern -- finally takes place, this can be a *powerful release of the energy that has been trapped in the problem pattern*, thus perhaps even a healing event.

It is how this release is navigated that determines the effects of this shedding in transition and death processes. Here again, we find that the change, transition, and death process can be navigated ever more consciously.

And here again, is the metaphor of death. Breaking a pattern is a dying. Are you prepared to release old patterns? Are you prepared to let old patterns die? Can you separate your self, your own identity, from the pattern or patterns you are releasing enough to let these patterns die while you survive? This release is a transcendence. Are you ready to transcend? Will you succeed? Can you change, transition, and die ever more consciously?

TRANSCENDING ONE'S PROGRAMMING

To do die well, to bring about a worthwhile living (in-life) transition or death, you must break your addiction to the programming that controls the pattern you are talking about changing or breaking.

ADVENTURES IN CHANGES, TRANSITIONS, AND DEATHS

Those concerned about chemical dependence, painful relationship patterns, chronic pain, life-threatening diseases, and other crises of one's programming are working with the same question -- how does one break out of one's addiction to one's own body's and mind's programming? What type of pattern death will you require to release -- to free – yourself from a problem pattern (or from a network of problem patterns)?

A significant difference between the obvious explicit and the more hidden implicit pattern addictions is that some addictions to programming are more subtle than others – may even design themselves to be more subtle and invisible than others.

The drug-addicted individual sees a physical thing, a drug, to which he or she is addicted. However, there may be countless other addictions embedded there.

And, individuals dealing with repeated problem emotional or physical health patterns often have no physical objects such as drugs onto which they can project or externalize their patterns. This makes the problem-process of problem addiction to one's programming very difficult to see, far more implicit.

The first step is to face the reality that addiction to both useful healthy patterns and problem unhealthy patterns takes place in all of us. Explicit addictions serve as great learning vehicles. They make the hidden components of pattern addiction much more apparent to us.

Implicit addictions are frequently discovered by people who are in recovery from explicit addictions such as drug/alcohol addictions, or sometimes even by those who are dealing with physical illnesses. These individuals become examples for all of us. They lead the way through the matrix of change, transition, and death into the realm of transcendence.

ADVENTURES IN CHANGES, TRANSITIONS, AND DEATHS

CONDITIONS FOR TRANSCENDENCE

Whether or not there is an effective and healthy death of a problem pattern relates to the *actualization of the transcendence*. And, transcendence is one of the most special experiences one can have during one's lifetime. Transcendence can be life healing.

Many of our problems are actually discovered, encountered, or created – in essence to generate the opportunity to transcend them, to heal our lives. As human beings we have a choice. We can either become so overwhelmed by our problems that we miss out on this amazing opportunity, or we can realize that pattern addiction is a *potential-laden* situation.

Those who are addicted to a pattern (of drug use or eating or something more subtle, such as an emotional or energetic pattern – or even a state of mind, a mind set) have a wonderful opportunity to experience transcendence --

specifically to transcend pattern addiction. Transcendence requires a new outlook on a situation. No matter how bleak and painful a situation may appear, it can be changed by being *RE-perceived.*

This means that, before any effective changes can occur, you must be convinced of the fact that *you can change or even let go of the problem pattern, that you <u>can</u> turn things around!*

You must believe in the possibility of your transcendence of problem patterning. You must also understand the phases and process of transcendence, which can be studied on an ongoing basis. No matter what level of understanding you reach, there is always more to be learned.

Remember, there is no such thing as a free lunch. The transcendence process requires *your commitment, your attention, your fortitude,* and *your faith* in the process. These are interactive states of mind.

ADVENTURES IN CHANGES, TRANSITIONS, AND DEATHS

REPEATABLE PHASES OF TRANSCENDENCE

Transcendence is a continuous and repeatable process through which an individual achieves elevation to a new level of awareness. (For many, this new level of awareness feels to be an ever higher spiritual plane.) There you will experience greater awareness and a higher degree of freedom. (Note that whether or not a person self-defines as being spiritual, the experience of overcoming or transcending a problem pattern can feel to be a spiritual experience, thus the *spiritual elevation* this chapter describes.)

For the sake of simplicity, to streamline this discussion, let's say here that the transcendence process is composed of four basic profound and repeatable phases (as in Figure 5.5), each of which is necessary for the process. These basic phases of transcendence are:

PRIMER FOR LIFE'S MINOR AND MAJOR CHALLENGES AND PASSAGES

> **Phase 1: -- Struggle** (see Figure 5.1)
>
> **Phase 2: -- Paradox** (see Figure 5.2)
>
> **Phase 3: -- Insight** (see Figure 5.3)
>
> **Phase 4: -- Spiritual Elevation** (see Figure 5.4)

Each phase has its own special characteristics. You will find basic diagrams of these phases on the pages of this chapter. As you examine each diagram, try to think generally here, thinking of your life in terms of these basic patterns. Make these diagrams part of your own mental imagery. Thinking about complex ideas in simple pictures often helps to learn about them on a deeper level.

Phase 1: Struggle

Every day we may struggle a little or a lot-- with other people, with family relationships, with work relationships, with ourselves, with morality, and maybe also with our cravings for drugs, with balancing our checkbooks, with heavy traffic, with our health, with our tempers, with our

ADVENTURES IN CHANGES, TRANSITIONS, AND DEATHS

moods, with living up to what we think we or others would like to see us live up to.

We often struggle without recognizing or seeing beyond the struggle, becoming so deeply caught up that it becomes impossible to step back and say, "Oh, I am struggling. This must be the first phase of transcendence." Yet, it is just this observation that will set us on the path to transcendence.

When we *are* struggling, we must take the time to tell ourselves that we *are struggling* -- and that seeing this struggle for what it is is good, because struggle is the first phase of transcendence.

You know what struggle feels like. Study Figure 5.1. This simple pattern diagram illustrates ups and downs, pushes and pulls, and highs and lows so typical of the struggling phase. During a true struggle, there must be low points in order for there to be high points -- both extremes are integral to it.

Figure 5.1.

Phase 2: Paradox

Paradox is a fantastic experience. Paradox can be painful. It can be frightening. It can be deadly. Paradox can produce a zombielike denial or avoidance or even numbness effect in those who experience it. Paradox is the experience of being in a situation from which there seems to be no escape, no resolution. The more powerful the paradox, the more of a trap it feels to be, the greater the release from it will be.

ADVENTURES IN CHANGES, TRANSITIONS, AND DEATHS

The person in paradox indeed feels trapped, often sees no exit. Energy trapped in paradox builds a valuable tension. That is, unless it is trapped too long, and then it stagnates and weakens, or bursts out of control into a dangerous runaway wobble.

Sometimes parents submit children to paradoxes in the form of double binds, something like this: "Which coat do you like?" a parent may ask a child. "The red coat or the blue one?" When the child then says, "The red coat," the parent says, "That's not a good choice, you should like the blue one." And then when the child says, "The blue one," the parent says, "Well, the red one is much better." When this happens, the child is experiencing a double bind: LOSE-LOSE. In this case, there is nothing the child can do that would be the right thing to elicit a positive response from the parent. The child is bound by unpleasant consequence no matter which choice he or she makes. There is no escape. The situation holds, or so it would seem, no real choices.

Some double binds come from outside us. However, most double binds come from within because we allow (or are forced to allow) ourselves to experience these as no exit situations, double binds. In living life, adults may at times create double bind situations for themselves with or without the help of other people.

For the child in the red coat / blue coat double bind above, release from the bind is seeing the folly of the parent's reasoning and not taking it personally. However, this is a large job for a child. All too often, children are forced into double bind situations, as are many adults.

Another double bind that many people find themselves trapped in is chemical dependence. The individual takes a drug to escape a painful, stressful, or boring situation. But the situation from which the person is trying to escape becomes even more painful, stressful, or boring when the person returns to it, as is inevitable upon coming down from the drug. While no escape is no escape, the drug escape is also no escape.

ADVENTURES IN CHANGES, TRANSITIONS, AND DEATHS

Paradoxes like this are extremely stressful and often painful. But faith in the transcendence process shows us that paradox serves a purpose. Without the tension, the feeling of being trapped in an unwinnable situation, there is no impetus for release, for moving on, for growing. The tension created by your paradoxes, when recognized and then used well, can generate enough energy for you to break out of them. You can learn to spot your paradoxes before they stagnate in order to harvest, to release, your valuable energy from them. Without the painful tenseness of paradox, you cannot experience the release -- the jump or shift in perception -- that is produced by breaking out of the paradox, the double bind.

Paradox is illustrated in Figure 5.2. Study this diagram for a few moments. This diagram shows the basic "standoff" or "holding pattern" in which people who need to let something of themselves die and to experience transcendence, get caught or even trap themselves. The only way out of this holding pattern is to break out of it and move on, to increase your perception so that you can see beyond the limits of the double bind that holds you there. The two arrows ending up against each other and going nowhere represent the forces that hold a pattern addicted person in his or her trap.

Figure 5.2

Paradox is a no exit sensation. Forces press against each other and hold the person stuck. One force is the powerful tendency to stay stuck, to stay pattern addicted, for example, to use drugs or relationships or work to avoid the stress and pain of staying stuck. The other is the stressful and painful effect of using that very something which is supposedly used to avoid stress and escape pain to do so.

ADVENTURES IN CHANGES, TRANSITIONS, AND DEATHS

This deadlock can hold you indefinitely in its grip. Or, if you choose to escape it, to transcend it, it can provide a take-off point into another level of awareness and a healing. As has been explained above, when the paradox of pattern addiction explodes, your energy is released. That fantastic energy can propel profound insight when harvested.

Whatever your pattern addictions may be, you can harness the energy found in their paradoxes, and then you can move -- fast forward -- into transcendence out those paradoxes. To do so, you must become highly alert to any tensions and other sensations you feel, and to whatever elements of your implicit pattern addictions may generate these.

Phase 3: Insight

Insight is a profound experience. But this insight often comes in small packages. Sometimes we experience insight without even realizing it. You may be driving along and

PRIMER FOR LIFE'S MINOR AND MAJOR CHALLENGES AND PASSAGES

suddenly grasp something about a problem that has been bothering you. Or you may be working -- perhaps on a scientific or a construction project -- and suddenly figure out an unexpected solution. All at once a new idea comes into your mind. You suddenly discover a new way of looking at a problem. This is an insight.

Insight is illustrated in Figure 5.3. Look at this simple figure for a while. This figure suggests the glimpse, or perception, of another way of seeing the world and of being in the world. The highest point in this diagram is this flash of realization. It represents a peek (and a peak) into a higher level of awareness.

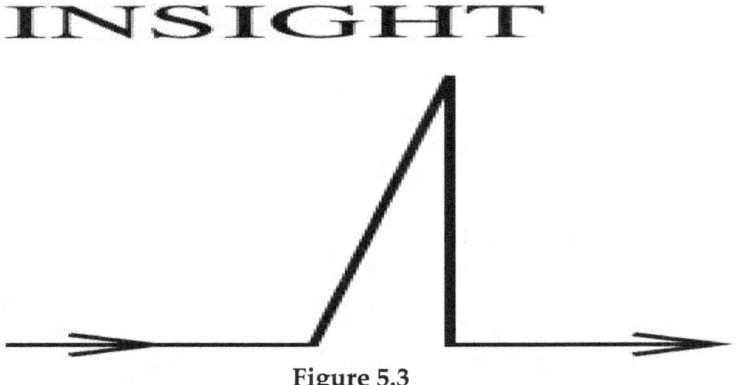

Figure 5.3

ADVENTURES IN CHANGES, TRANSITIONS, AND DEATHS

Now, notice that the line falls back, or almost back, to its original level. This is because insight, this leap in awareness, is a temporary jump in perception. This insight itself does not automatically bring growth. In order to grow, insight must be recognized and sustained. When it is, spiritual elevation becomes reality.

Phase 4: Elevation

Elevation, or what we can also call spiritual elevation, is illustrated in Figure 5.4. Gaze at this figure a moment. What does this diagram symbolize to you? This pattern signifies a jump in perception. This jump is actually an insight that is *sustained.*

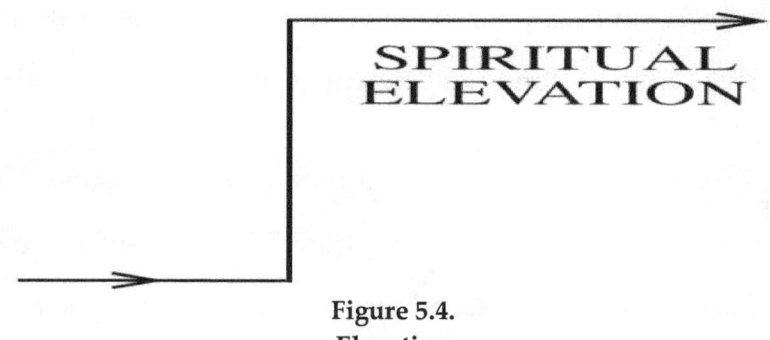

Figure 5.4.
Elevation

The self, the soul, the spirit, rises to a new level of awareness, of being, and maintains this. This "holding on" is best described as the experience of *sustained insight*. Without being sustained, the insight is usually bright and brief and dropping back to or close to the original, pre-insight, way of seeing and being in the world, as was seen in Figure 5.3. Spiritual elevation differs from insight in that there is no going back to one's previous perceptions.

From the new level of awareness achieved by spiritual elevation, each of the phases of transcendence may have to be repeated in order to reach the next level of spiritual elevation. One can always discover new struggles, paradoxes, and insights to generate further awareness and spiritual growth – and new elevation of the SELF.

This exciting and adventurous process of transcendence is suggested in Figure 5.5. This figure shows the four phases of transcendence linked together. The cycle of these four linked phases is repeatable, with some phases

ADVENTURES IN CHANGES, TRANSITIONS, AND DEATHS

repeated several times each cycle, as in Figure 5.7. Contemplate these diagrams for a while.

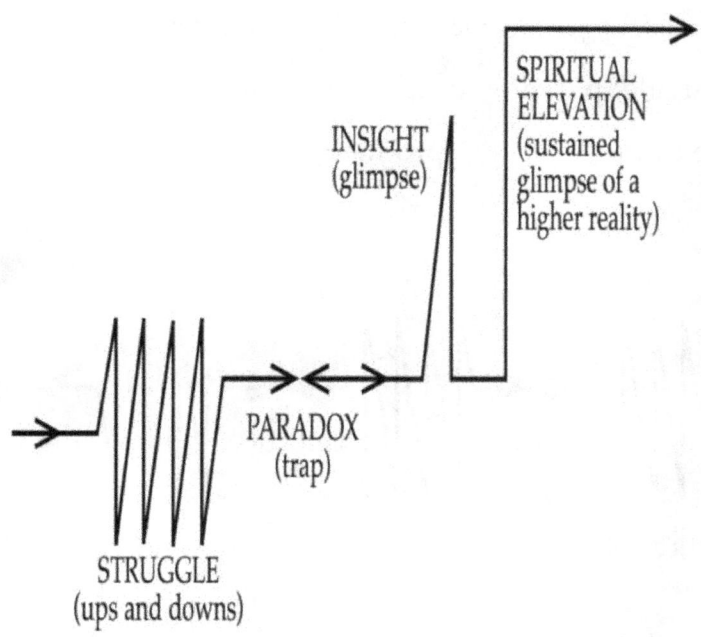

**Figure 5.5.
Adventures in Transcendence**

Be certain that you understand that each phase may take barely a few seconds or last for years. Some people struggle all their lives. Others live in a perpetual stage of paradox. Some rotate between struggle and paradox, as Figure 5.6 demonstrates. Being more consciously aware of the overall patterns we can be caught in or moving through -- struggle, paradox, insight, and elevation -- can help us move through these in productive ways.

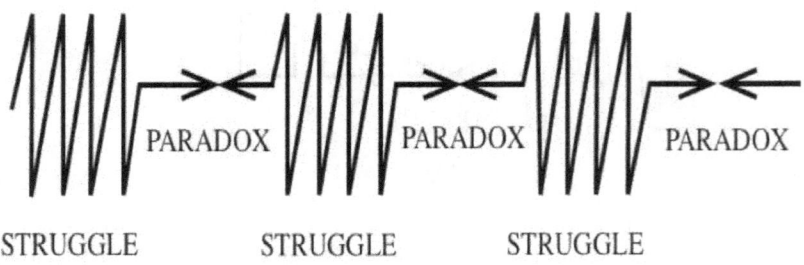

Figure 5.6.
Struggle Paradox Struggle Paradox

ADVENTURES IN CHANGES, TRANSITIONS, AND DEATHS

Perhaps some people reach a final spiritual elevation at (or in the process of) physical death. However, in living daily life, many people have insights, but do not recognize or sustain these. Thus they continuously return to the same old paradoxes that may have fueled these insights. Or they fall back into the struggles that may have fueled these paradoxes.

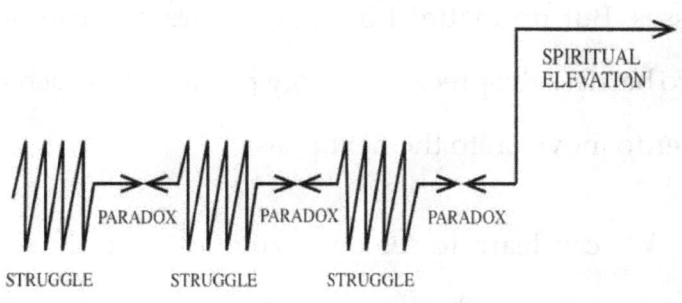

Figure 5.7.
Struggle And Paradox Into Elevation

PRIMER FOR LIFE'S MINOR AND MAJOR CHALLENGES AND PASSAGES

Each of us follows his or her own life pattern. However, no one's pattern is written in stone. Ideally, we could be taught as children to recognize the four basic patterns identified in this chapter as phases of transcendence – and of course to know what the ongoing process of transcendence itself is about. Then, as adults, it would be much easier for us to see where we are in our processes and to take more conscious control of these processes. But no matter how old we are, we can always learn to harness the precious energy produced in each phase in order to move on to the next phase.

We can learn to see our struggles as fertile ground for astounding growth. We can learn to appreciate paradox, recognize insight, and strive for spiritual elevation. If you keep trying to see – to sensitize to -- the patterns in your life, you will eventually understand that you are already on the path of transcendence. The gifts of life and death will then be clear to you. Your struggles are important stepping stones. Respect your struggles.

ADVENTURES IN CHANGES, TRANSITIONS, AND DEATHS

BASIC IDEAS FOR TRANSCENDING ONE'S PATTERNING

We have been examining the concept of transcendence -- what it is, and what it takes to achieve it. The concept can be applied to any obstacle or difficulty we encounter, whether it be emotional, financial, physical, or another type of issue or problem.

NOTE THAT

1. Addiction to a pattern is a powerful bondage that can only be broken by something more powerful. One must accept this as a fact and appreciate the size and seriousness of the task of breaking pattern addiction.

2. Pattern addiction can be very subtle and difficult to recognize. Therefore some individuals either present themselves, or are presented, with the challenge of an explicit addiction so that they may recognize how addicted to patterning we all are. They then undergo

the struggle to break out of their most explicit addictive patterns and, in the process of that struggle, experience growth. Some people have found the recognition of addiction to be their primary opportunity for growth. Drug, alcohol, food, spending, and gambling addictions are some of the easiest patterns to spot and thus offer some of the most accessible opportunity to practice transcendence and to grow.

3. Whether or not we exhibit any explicit addictions, we all are pattern addicts. Pattern addiction is a healthy function, yet too frequently pattern addiction runs far awry.

4. The ultimate form of learning is transcendence, a process composed of four basic and repeating phases: struggle, paradox, insight, and spiritual elevation. This overall four phase process is a repetitive, never-

ADVENTURES IN CHANGES, TRANSITIONS, AND DEATHS

ending process, and each phase within this process is itself going to be repeated many times.

5. Your entire experience of living and of dying large and small deaths is transformed the moment you identify the phase of the process you are currently experiencing.

6. One way to promote insight, spiritual elevation, and thus transcendence is through the pain, struggle, and paradox of problem pattern addiction. Problem pattern-addicted individuals tend to *select* their particular expressions of addiction -- their explicit addictions -- to alert themselves to their deeper addictions.

7. Remember that the transcendence we are describing is a process that gains power as it progresses. Progressive transcendence can overcome pattern

addiction and then move beyond. *There is no end point to this process.*

8. One must *work* to maintain the insights and spiritual elevations gained in the process of transcendence.

9. With every full cycle of transcendence comes an entirely new way of seeing the self and the world. Be ready and open to total change and new life – and then to move into the next cycle.

ONGOING TRANSCENDENCE

Only an ongoing commitment to awareness and transcendence can truly heal the wounds to the soul that are caused by our programmed-in pattern addictions. And only massive transcendence will heal the world. As the human species becomes more aware of its ability to consciously choose to transcend the trap of patterning in the physical world, it will expand to further include the realm of the

ADVENTURES IN CHANGES, TRANSITIONS, AND DEATHS

spirit. We begin to see that biological death is not the only means of such transcendence.

Our ongoing everyday transcendence process
is always taking place
once we begin to see this.

PRIMER FOR LIFE'S MINOR AND MAJOR CHALLENGES AND PASSAGES

ADVENTURES IN CHANGES, TRANSITIONS, AND DEATHS

6
Mapping Your Transitions And Deaths

> *As we draw ourselves to ever more awareness of our change, transition, and death processes, even of the patterns involved in these processes, we see that we can indeed be not only ever more consciously aware of our patterns, but also where needed, <u>consciously move through and beyond these patterns</u>.*
>
> *We begin to see that the paths we follow in our lives have energetic, even thematic, characteristics. We can map our patterns and processes of living, even of change, transition, and death. As we begin to map these processes, we see how every process has its own characteristics such as tempo, intensity, etc. Yet, these processes also have remarkable similarities we can be ever more aware of.*

Notice where you are and how you feel. Find yourself in the process of living and dying. Can you map your life? Can you map any of your living transitions and deaths? How about the roads leading up to those changes, transitions, and deaths, deaths of patterns and deaths of passages, even of lives? Of course, the general process of transcendence toward lasting elevation (here below in Figure 6.1.) is a general map (as first suggested in Figure 5.5, last chapter).

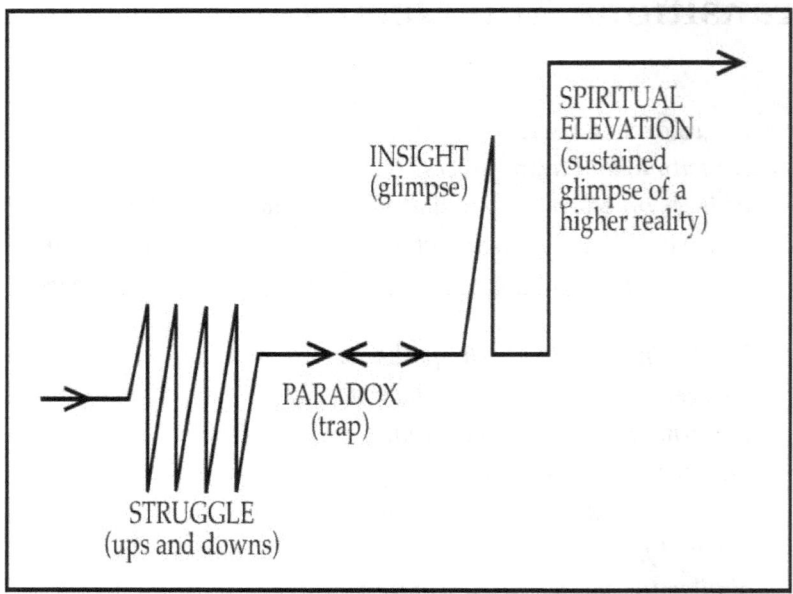

Figure 6.1

Four Repeatable and Intermixable Phases

ADVENTURES IN CHANGES, TRANSITIONS, AND DEATHS

KEY IN YOUR ELEVATING BEYOND PRESENT PATTERNS

You can become increasingly aware of the sensations involved here. Many times, we are not attaching words to what we are feeling and sensing, and therefore we are not fully aware, not consciously noticing what is happening within and around us. Here is where we can learn to effectively sense and visualize what may or may not have fully or adequately been put into words, or enough words, in our minds. Here is where we can *visually map* our situations, give an image to the energy patterns we sense we are stuck in or moving through, or want to move through.

You can begin to read the map of your life. You can begin to map your life processes, as you become ever more aware of what at first may seem to be invisible or very subtle situations and energy arrangements. This is key in pulling into conscious awareness more and more of your processes of change, transition, and death. Ultimately, this increased

PRIMER FOR LIFE'S MINOR AND MAJOR CHALLENGES AND PASSAGES

awareness can be key in surviving both here and beyond where you are now. This can be key in generating the elevation, the transcendence, you seek.

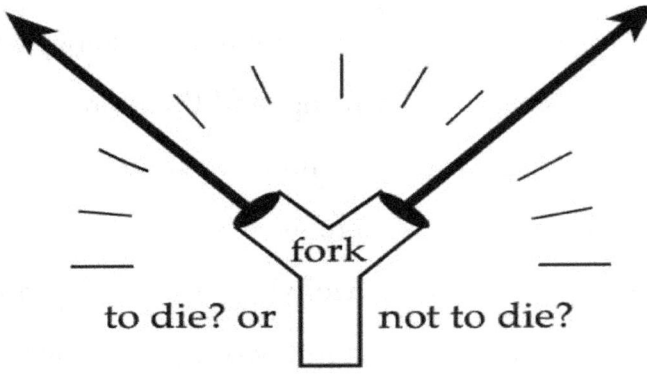

**Figure 6.2.
The Fork In The Road**

RECOGNIZE THE FORK IN THE ROAD THERE AMONG THE STUCK PATTERNS

There are times when life brings you to a fork in your road. Sometimes, you don't see the fork coming. It just appears. Sometimes you don't realize that the fork has appeared, or that you are straddling the forked road and feeling the **im**-balancing tug of conflicting choices. Do you

ADVENTURES IN CHANGES, TRANSITIONS, AND DEATHS

move on or stay stuck, trapped? Do you choose to change or not, to transition or not, to let a pattern die or not?

NAVIGATE THE STUCK EXPERIENCE

When you feel substantially unsettled for a significant chunk of time (whatever time that may be for you), take a look under your feet. Try to see where you are in your life. There, a choice to go one way or another -- to take one course of action or another -- can be made.

It is as if this choice is offering itself to you, revealing itself to you. Of course, this is you revealing this to yourself. However you sense this, you begin to know that something small or large, minor or major, must be left behind, no matter how difficult or painful.

You may know all this and still not be able to move forward. You may feel that there are no good options. You may can feel that you cannot make a change. There can be a holding pattern, a trap for that matter....

PRIMER FOR LIFE'S MINOR AND MAJOR CHALLENGES AND PASSAGES

→ → → stuck, trapped ← ← ←

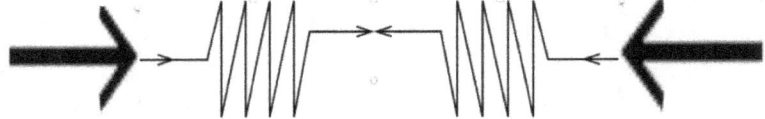

Figure 6.3.
NO EXIT
PARADOX
ENERGY TRAP

Here, you may feel some hesitation or confusion, maybe also some stress or even anguish, in that you sense you have to make a choice to either leave the paradox or to stay stuck. You may also feel that if you choose to exit the paradox, you will perhaps need to choose which path to follow out of the paradox. Here is that fork in the road.

Take a moment here, as you can even rejoice because you are actually at the junction we can call THE NO EXIT PARADOX ENERGY TRAP. Look closely, sense clearly

ADVENTURES IN CHANGES, TRANSITIONS, AND DEATHS

what energetic situation you are experiencing. Here you find you do have THE ESCAPE FROM PARADOX OPTION. The energy trapped in a paradox, in a double bind, is moving you toward the option of release, moving you right there to the fork in the road. And then, this energy can be released in the escape. This is actually you moving you.

How do you see this? How do you let yourself move ahead now? If the situation feels too large for you to manage, then look for even a tiny baby step in the direction of a path out, find a very minor change to start. This can move the energy forward without the experience being all at once too intense.

However minor or major the choice you set for yourself may be, make a choice to move forward to exit the stuck place, even if this is just a little bit forward. Move yourself into a commitment to go one way or the other, to take one road or another out of the trap. You can always change to a new road if the one you choose now is not the one you prefer later.

It is time to consciously and clearly choose to go further with the developments already forming in the fork, or choose to go back to the perhaps deceptive illusion of the safer, seemingly "saner" life within the paradox. (This sounds odd, but it is actually less work to stay trapped than to break out. However, once out, you are much freer.)

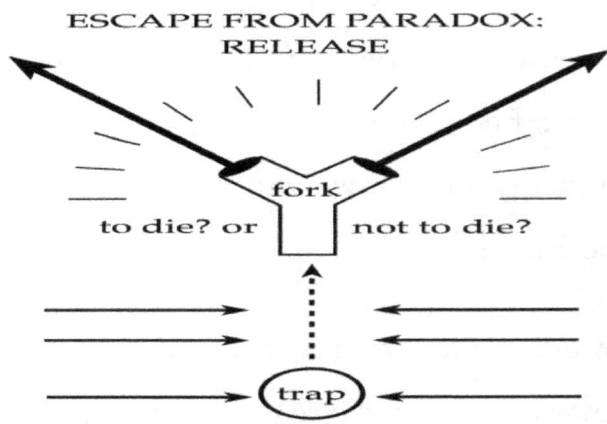

Figure 6.4.
The Release

ADVENTURES IN CHANGES, TRANSITIONS, AND DEATHS

UNDERSTAND THE SENSE OF INSTABILITY

Be aware, sensitize to the situation you are moving through. As you move toward escape from the trap of paradox, you may feel intensely unsettled. Either you or the world around you may feel unbudging, rigid, even stuck, while at the same time verging on chaotic, out of order. You may have no sense that things will ever look quite the same again. And you know that if you commit to escape, things may indeed never look the same again.

And so, as you move toward the change, toward your growth and survival, you destabilize your trap, your beat at the doors of your paradox. Things may indeed become somewhat or even highly unstable. This is exactly that state of readiness for change that any system, including that of a living organism (such as you are) has to reach to evolve beyond its present level of development.

But what finally opens, loosens, an extremely rigid trap? The more rigid the trap is, the more energy is required to hold it in place.

Some kind of minor or major psychophysical shock, perhaps a small or large catastrophe, a small or large calamity, may be required to motivate, propel, loosen up a rigid system.

HEAR YOUR VOICE

About the time the tension crescendos, you may, if you listen, hear a voice in your head. Do not be alarmed. It will not harm you. This is likely your higher self-talking, speaking to you from the deeper dimensions of yourself.

Become more sensitive to the subtle inputs you give yourself as you get ready to let a minor or major part of your life or part of your behavior change or die. Pay attention to very quiet hints, murmurs in your mind that you would have normally missed or totally ignored. These inputs may

ADVENTURES IN CHANGES, TRANSITIONS, AND DEATHS

contribute to your seeming unbalancing, in that you feel a bit disturbed, maybe even a little crazy. But fear not. You are right where you should be.

USE YOUR IMAGINATION
AS YOU MOVE THROUGH

Listen to yourself here. You may sense you hear or feel a voice guiding you. You may be transducing, reducing the frequency of the transmissions from your higher self – or perhaps let's say from your subconscious -- to a frequency that your mind can consciously receive and use.

By being aware of this process, you can decide to gain some control over your mind's receiving mechanisms. You will begin to pick up a wider band of information from yourself and the world around you. (Refer to the discussion and application of what this book series defines as *metacognitive awareness* in other books in this series. See Recommended Reading listed in the APPENDICES section of this present book.)

PRIMER FOR LIFE'S MINOR AND MAJOR CHALLENGES AND PASSAGES

SEE MORE, SENSE MORE

This widening of your band of perception is a marvelous advancement in your own awareness of your own situation, and of your own self, consciousness, soul. Still, at first, even if you are sensitive enough, practiced enough, and willing enough to hear your own voice, you (or your brain or your society) may question somewhat or even deny the experience.

This is not surprising. Such evolution, especially for we poor souls who may have not been instructed in the process, can be excruciatingly disorienting. To help you with this, you are now being instructed in an introductory subtle and gentle manner. Relax. The excruciation may fade before the disorientation. However, eventually, both will recede.

Remember, your mind's own imagination and visualization tools can be key in your ever more consciously navigating your change, transition, and death processes.

ADVENTURES IN CHANGES, TRANSITIONS, AND DEATHS

MAP YOUR LIFE

As you undergo any transition, make yourself a map, or even several maps. Draw these maps and keep these handy. In fact, it can be most helpful to always be sketching maps of your processes. This helps pull more and more of your conscious awareness in to your life and its processes of change, transition, and death. Be ready to revise or add on to your map or maps as you continue on into the journey, the adventure of life and death, this amazing journey you have begun.

The following maps represent a few change, transition, and dying processes, whether these be in daily life, or in larger life stages (such as aging, or relating, or divorcing, or dealing with health issues, etc.), or in end-of-life stages, or for some, even in after-life processes.

Except for Figure 6.1, which was previously explained, these maps are for you to explain to your self.

This is your own teaching. Study these. Attempt to describe a process of change, of transition, of dying that fits each map. Then think of a few major changes in your life and map the processes leading up to, moving through, and leaving each of these transitions.

NOTE THAT THE FOLLOWING ARE SAMPLE MAPS

- **Figure 6.5. Death Release Map:**

This map depicts a process of moving between struggle and insight several times, bouncing back into struggle each time the insight is not sustained. When the insight is not sustained, the elevation does not happen.

A sort of stuck situation or paradox develops when there feels to be no moving out of this back and forth status. Yet, the *LEAP out* or *death release* from the paradox can be navigated, can generate the elevation from itself. This can be what can also be called *the transcendence out of* this trap or stuck situation.

ADVENTURES IN CHANGES, TRANSITIONS, AND DEATHS

- **Figure 6.6. Untrained Death Release Map:**

  As this figure indicates, we can move or bounce back and forth among stages and patterns of change, transition, and death. When we are <u>not alert</u> to the stages we are moving through, and what the energies are that tell us about the stages we are moving through, we may find ourselves unsure how to move beyond stages and their patterns. We may therefore be unaware of, or confused by, or even trapped in, the process.

- **Figure 6.7. Energy Loss Map:**

  This figure suggests that remaining caught in traps and paradoxes for extended periods of time can drain the energy trapped there. This is energy that we might otherwise be able to release to ourselves to propel positive movements into elevations from, transcendences of, problem situations and patterns.

- **Figure 6.8. Profound Release Map:**

This figure indicates that there is the option of ever more consciously navigating through struggles, paradoxes, insights, and elevations we encounter in our change, transition, and death processes. Again and again, we can work toward renewed elevations where our processes are productive.

ADVENTURES IN CHANGES, TRANSITIONS, AND DEATHS

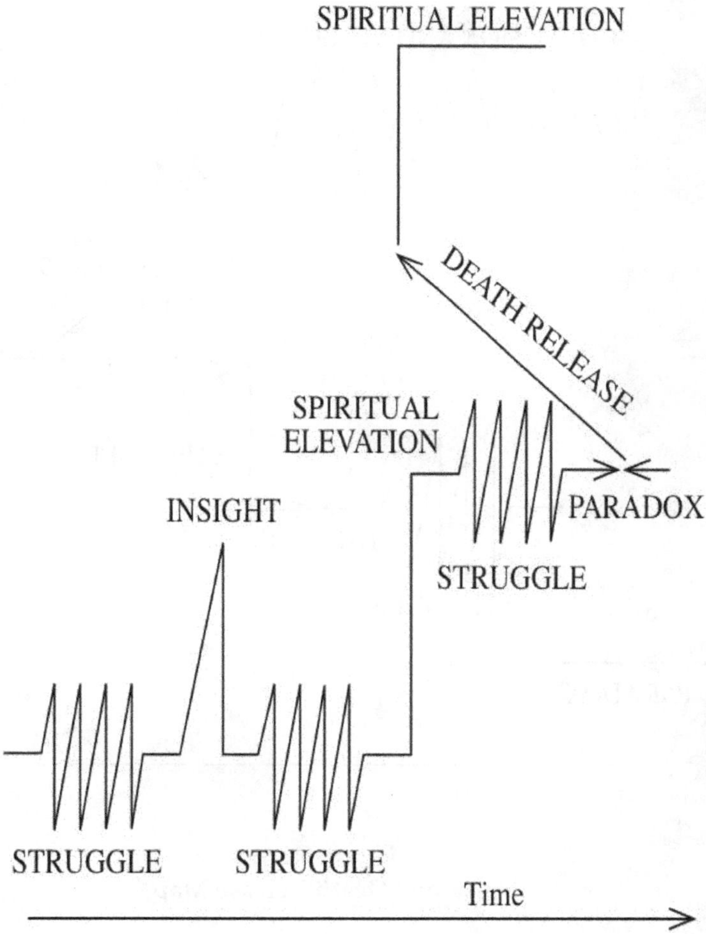

Figure 6.5.
Death Release Map

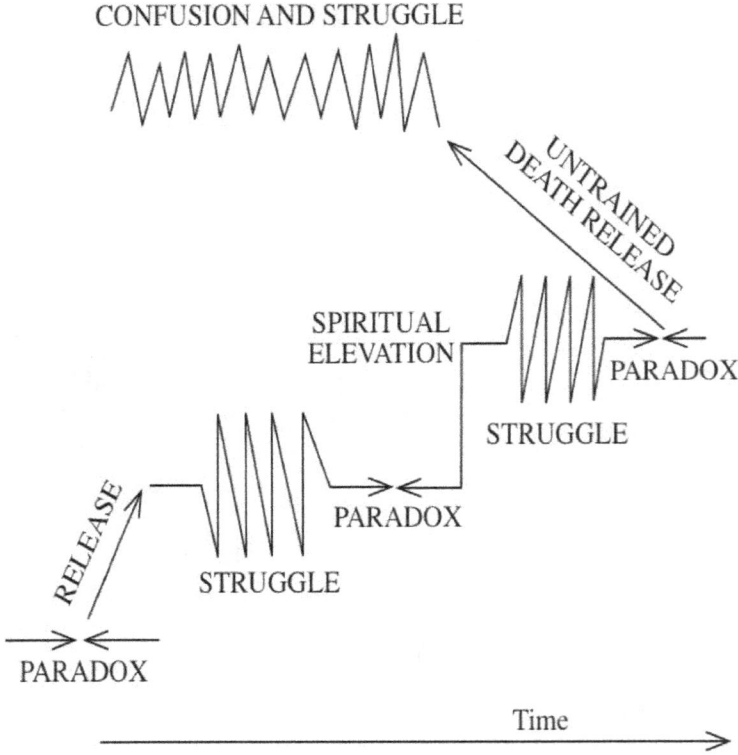

**Figure 6.6.
Untrained Death Release Map**

ADVENTURES IN CHANGES, TRANSITIONS, AND DEATHS

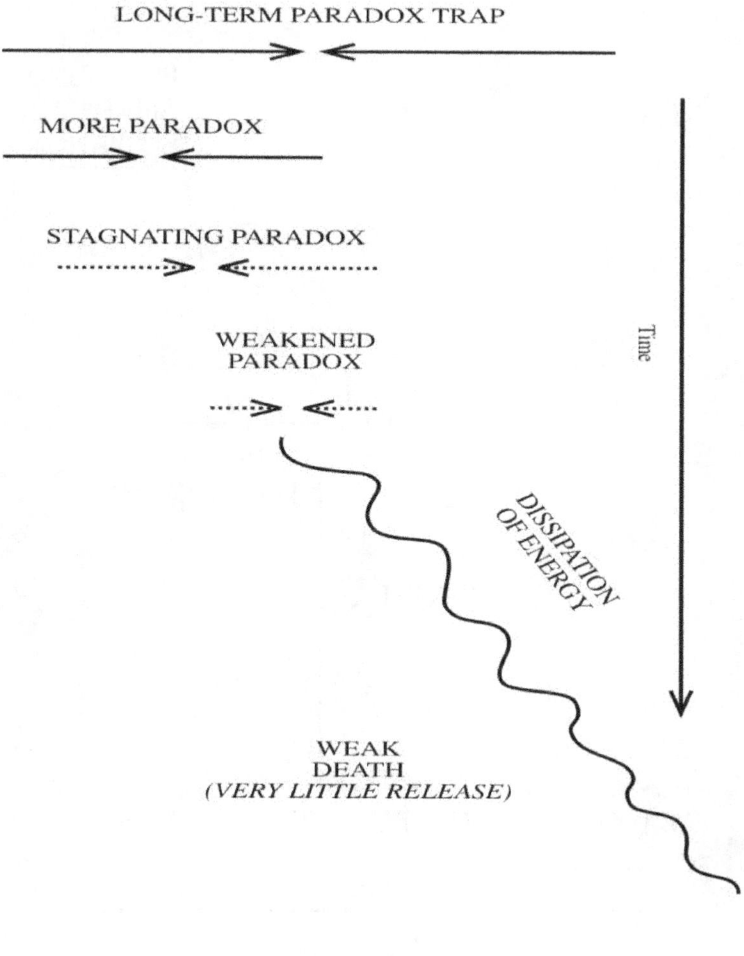

**Figure 6.7.
Energy Loss Map**

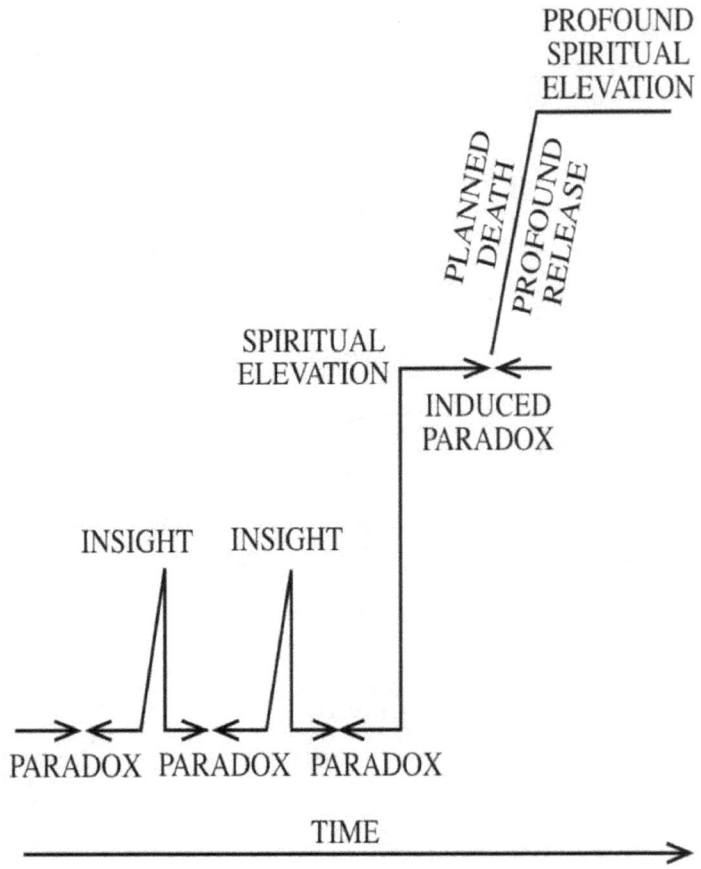

Figure 6.8
Profound Release Map

ADVENTURES IN CHANGES, TRANSITIONS, AND DEATHS

7
Transitions From One Dimension Of Your Reality To Another

How we see our in-life as well as seeming end-of-life, and perhaps even after-life, changes, transitions, and deaths, affects how we move through – and survive -- these change, transition, and death processes. Understanding ourselves as having a range of dimensions of SELF gives us the opportunity to be creative in our thinking here, to imagine or even visualize what moving through and surviving can feel like.

We can understand that the internal <u>realities we define and design for ourselves are ours</u>. These cannot be taken away from us. The elements and <u>dimensions of our own consciousness, our personal realm</u>, that we generate for ourselves can be <u>key in our successful navigation and surviving of our changes, transitions, and deaths</u>.

This book suggests that you take in and pull together some ancient and some modern teachings, along with the

new ideas being shared on these pages. Some of this material is a rethinking of medicine and psychology, some of this is a slightly different perspective on politics. Much of this material is pressing the edges of what we know, or of what we have been allowed to know about who and what we are.

On the pages of this book (and of all the books in this KEYS TO CONSCIOUSNESS AND SURVIVAL SERIES) you will find both a re-framing and a re-defining of the concepts: of death; of transition and change as forms of death: of in-life transitions and changes as in-life lessons on death; and, of the options at death and BEYOND.

Elements of this material will perhaps be described by some as "esoteric" teaching. Esoteric is generally defined as teaching reserved for the so-called select few, the "eso-" or inner circle. Esoteric has generally been defined as the opposite of exoteric, exoteric being teaching somewhat altered or reduced down for the so-called many, for the "exo-" or outer circle.

ADVENTURES IN CHANGES, TRANSITIONS, AND DEATHS

However, what we can see here is that we can access – *and indeed have a right to access* -- our own wisdom regarding what lies BEYOND our everyday reality, at least the everyday reality we are told to believe is so-called "real." (For more on this matter of what we are told is real about what may lie BEYOND, Readers are encouraged to see other volumes in this series, such as Volume 7, KEYS TO ACCESSING THE BEYOND.)

WHY THIS ESOTERIC DISCUSSION

Here, let's think in terms of what may have once been regarded by some political and spiritual leaders as forbidden knowledge. These were ideas and concepts reserved for the so-called privileged, or for the leaders themselves – as accessing this knowledge was said to bring a personal and perhaps even political power that some of those in control may have sought to reserve for themselves. (Again, for more on these matters, refer to other books in this series, such as KEYS TO ACCESSING THE BEYOND,

Volume 7, and the HOW TO DIE AND SURVIVE books, Volumes 4, 11, and 14.)

Here, in this present book, you are being invited to rethink death because you are a far more potent being than most teachers of history, science, and religion may have told you you are. You are so expansive a being that your own personal consciousness already touches many states of reality, many arrangements of energy, many dimensions of being. In fact, what you seek to access is already right here.

RIGHT HERE

Right here? You may wonder where else you could really be while you are right here. "Right here" is an elusive concept, even though it sounds concrete. In reality, there is no more of a right here here than there is anywhere else. Basically, the (of course valuable in daily life) sense of location you have is affected by your (or your brain's) tie to your physical biological reality.

ADVENTURES IN CHANGES, TRANSITIONS, AND DEATHS

However, this location-sense is only one concept, just one conceptual dimension, of your existence. There are many other dimensions or arrangements or concepts of self, of personal energy arrangements, and of reality. Those dimensions are already all "right here." This is true because you, everyone, exists in a matrix of intersecting so-called dimensions with varying degrees of physicality and non-physicality *(or as some will say, with varying degrees of validity, as the non-physical realm of your existence, and of your imagination/visualization functions that are developing this realm, are difficult to measure and prove scientifically here on this 3-D physical Earth plane).*

You are always sensing and determining what you sense about your own reality. The dimensions of your reality are yours to define and design within your mind and consciousness.

Note: At this point in my presentation of this material, some members of my audiences ask me, "But then, why

can't I see these other dimensions of my SELF?" The answer is that you can see these so-called dimensions as concepts, as ideas, as places in your mind and consciousness, although not the way you usually see things.

You will see much more when you add to, expand upon, what your physical biological eyes see, when you see that your biological eyes are not the only and ultimate arbiters of your own reality. You can retrain and extend your optic nerve and develop your third eye. Everything is right here whether or not you can see it at this time.

THE DIMENSIONS OF YOUR REALITY

Everyday life has many faces. Even within the seemingly limited realities in which many of us believe we live, there are many realities. Energy is always arranging and rearranging here and everywhere. Even your *idea of your own personal energy* re-defines itself as you -- or at least your imagination -- leaves or extends, reaches BEYOND, what you feel is your own physicality. Perhaps energy is no

ADVENTURES IN CHANGES, TRANSITIONS, AND DEATHS

longer the word for what this energy becomes out there BEYOND the reality you believe you are presently living in. Give this a bit of time. You will begin to see more of your mind's sense of your own non-physicality.

Take some time to think of even biological death as an actual transition rather than an ending. Let the concept become a part of you. Think of death as a transition, yes, a relocation of your SELF, of your personal energy field, moving or expanding from one reality into another, from one dimension of your SELF to another.

You can make such a transition or relocation of your own personal self and energy arrangement with clarity, whatever the level of transition may be, whether it is a transition out of a personal belief system, or out a stage of life, or perhaps out a relationship, out of a drug addiction, out of an illness -- or out of a physical body in the case of biological death. Think of all your in-life, seeming end-of-life, and perhaps even after-life changes as being transitions, shifts, from one state of your reality to another.

You are designing your own realm BEYOND, for current exploration and perhaps future occupation. This is about rethinking the nature of your reality, when and where ever you are. This is about your becoming ever more aware of your interdimensional nature as you deal with your daily life, even later end-of-life, and perhaps also after-life situations.

The following discussion may help loosen any rigid perceptions of reality that may keep you (or your controlling biological brain) from knowing this. Allow these ideas to flow into your mentality without working at taking them in.

Remember that this discussion is basically telling you that you can ever more consciously rearrange your **idea of yourself, of your reality, of what we still call your energy.**

ADVENTURES IN CHANGES, TRANSITIONS, AND DEATHS

You can amend, move away from, and or break, any pattern addiction or energy pattern in which you are trapped.

You can be ever more aware of your SELF as a personal life force, as a being independent of what both <u>the physical reality you live in</u> -- and <u>the programming of your biological brain</u> -- seek to hold you to. Strive for this independence of SELF, this independence of how you see your actual SELF, as this is who actually survives. Stay with your actual SELF, get to know your actual SELF more every day.

This is about your survival as your own personal life force.

Yes, this is your personal life force we are talking about here.

**This is <u>your own</u> personal identity,
<u>your own</u> personal life force.
You can see this force and define this force
and then free your SELF
<u>to survive.</u>**

PRIMER FOR LIFE'S MINOR AND MAJOR CHALLENGES AND PASSAGES

8
The LEAP Of Faith In Your SELF

By now, it is clear that this book looks at death as part of a long line of changes and transitions -- and at changes and transitions as models, even training grounds, for minor and major death experiences. In again and again finding our way through these experiences, we can begin to recognize general landmarks, revealing direction signs, indicators telling us where and who we are, where and which part of ourselves or our patterns and energy arrangements may go which way when.

There is no single take-off point in this discussion. Every step of the way, you will find new avenues of your SELF to explore. You are imagining that you are opening to a place where the laws of the physical world do not apply. Here you are free to explore what you may not have been invited to know or see before. This is the realm of own your mind, of your own SELF. This is your own territory where you can define your change, transition, and death processes as you wish to. You can define your survival as a consciousness as you wish to. Your LEAP of faith here is in your SELF. Know that you indeed have a SELF who can learn to navigate and survive change, transition, and death processes both here and BEYOND.

Consider for a moment thinking of yourself as an energy formation, a non-physical self, who can move at will around space and time. Use your imagination.

IMAGINATION IS A KEY TOOL HERE

Here is the frontier of the SELF, of your SELF, of your own personal consciousness, of your own personal domain. We can imagine the realm of what may be the after-life as a non-physical place we may be able to go into as beings who no longer have physical biological bodies. Give yourself some time to experience your imagination exploring these ideas.

You are indeed imagining that you are opening to a place where the laws of the physical world do not apply. Here you are free to imagine, visualize, explore what you may not have been invited to know or see before.

This is the realm of your own mind, of your own SELF. This is your own territory where you can define

ADVENTURES IN CHANGES, TRANSITIONS, AND DEATHS

your own change, transition, and death processes – your own survival – as you wish to.

**You can define
your own survival as a personal consciousness
as you wish to.**

Dedicated athletes practice almost daily. They prepare themselves to move their bodies in efficient, rewarding, and successful ways. Here, we are not talking about physical body exercise, yet we are talking about exercising the mind, the awareness.

Yes, you can exercise your mind, such as your imagination and visualization and concentration skills, to help you bring efficiency and success, and rewards, to your minor and major change, transition, and death processes.

See yourself as highly mobile. Visualize yourself moving through your out-of-body reality. After all, this is a state you may at some time find yourself in, whether in your dreams, or perhaps in your near death experiences, or perhaps during and following your biological dying processes -- yes, here and BEYOND.

IMAGERY CAN ASSIST TRANSITION

So allow your imagination to explore the idea of moving BEYOND your present day patterns and realities. Give this a few moments.

Notice that, if you wish to, you can shrink down or evaporate (your choice) and pass through what feels to the mind to be something like the eye of the needle, and then expand right into the release and relief of what may seem to be heaven.

You can come and go from that heaven, to and from that sort of hyperspace, to and from other dimensions of yourself, other vibrational levels of your reality, anytime

ADVENTURES IN CHANGES, TRANSITIONS, AND DEATHS

you choose. It is your right to be able to move your self, your mind, your soul, around this way.

MOVE THROUGH TO ANOTHER STATE OF SELF

Think of this *passing through* as a way to survive change, transition, and or biological death while being who you actually are, while being your actual SELF. After all, this actual SELF is who can survive even a challenging transition such as one that could be faced during disaster or death. In a passage that may feel like death, you may sense you can pass right through the so-called eye of the needle into another state of mind, dimension of your SELF, of your reality.

In fact, disaster, calamity, apocalypse, whether it is an apocalypse which is all in your mind or a natural disaster such as an earthquake, is often the reason for reaching through the imagined eye toward the beyond. The beyond is, simply, a place where your sense of self, your being, can be free of the detrimental patterns trapping it – free to survive.

MOVING THROUGH DIMENSIONS OF SELF

Recall the earlier discussion of how important it is to generally sense, know, when you are at a choice point, a fork in the road. (See again Figure 6.4.) It is equally important to be able to detect the openings to opportunities – the doors into passages -- these eyes of these needles -- these windows into other realities, other states of mind, of self. Your passages, pathways, are all around you yet may remain hidden out of your conscious awareness, deep in your sub- and even un- conscious realms until you train yourself to see or sense them.

With practice, you will find your windows of opportunity. Think of these as openings to other parts of your mind or consciousness. Yes, think of these windows as your own windows of opportunity -- although they may appear at first, if you can spot them at all, to be escape

ADVENTURES IN CHANGES, TRANSITIONS, AND DEATHS

hatches. You can move through these windows by imagining or actually becoming what you visualize as being very very small or compact, or so very spread out, vast, that you have no physical density.

Remember that you can in your mind's eye (or in your imagination) become very dense – shrink into a sort of *no-whereness*, or spread very thin – expand into a sort of *every-whereness*. Seeing your self as able to move in and out of states of mind, of awareness, is up to you. This sense of mobility – of survival -- is your choice. You can, at any moment that you have, employ visualization and imagination techniques to open your third eye (so to speak). Just think yourself into the form you choose. Imagination is quite powerful in this way.

SENSING YOUR SELF MOVING
THROUGH DIMENSIONS OF SELF

Moving the self from one dimension of your own personal territory, your own personal reality, to another is

itself a form of death -- in that you are moving or shifting out of patterns. All death, including living death in which there is no physical death, can be compared to this pattern-shifting pattern-exiting process.

As you feel you are shifting your reality or environment, you may find a range of sensations or perceptions coming to you. <u>This is you sensitizing yourself</u> to the shifting realities you are experiencing as you move through your transitions.

For example, you may feel you are traveling through sheets of glass, gently shattering each of them as you move -- and then being propelled by the force of that shattering still deeper through the glass sheets, which continue to shatter or perhaps melt as you proceed.

You may very briefly wonder whether you are drowning out there. You are not. You can recall this discussion here and know you are not. Any sense you may have, such as feeling you are at the bottom of a lake or a sea,

ADVENTURES IN CHANGES, TRANSITIONS, AND DEATHS

rapidly, even instantaneously, evaporates. For just a moment, you may think you cannot see anything. Then right away your new eyes open.

If you find yourself amidst such an experience, let time pass, which it will do momentarily, again even instantaneously. After a while, you may feel you sense or see flat slabs of light fly out of the dark, like new pieces of soft floating broken glass. Imagine that you become one of those pieces of broken glass. ***Let yourself softly shatter.*** Feel you are breaking apart from your holding pattern, from your previously rigid or even stuck pattern structure.

If you feel no immediate relief when you dissolve here, hang on another brief moment. Let yourself be flat -- but take on a fluidity to your flatness: perhaps sense that you are floating there in the surface of a body of water, the top of the lake or sea. Sense that you are accepting, or at least sensing, your reduction to a two dimensional form for just a little while.

PRIMER FOR LIFE'S MINOR AND MAJOR CHALLENGES AND PASSAGES

While you are sensing your momentary reduction to a two dimensional form, you will remember this description. You will know that the intense flatness, the compression you feel, is merely a quickly passing state (unless you do, of your own free will, choose to stay in that compressed form).

Should you have such an experience, you are sensing yourself passing through the flatness of two dimensional reality, where everything exists on a plane. However, even as this is happening to you, you may cling to your earthly views of 3-D physical plane reality.

You may have no sense that you are compressing in order to launch yourself. In terms of cross-dimensional travel, you can say that you are launching yourself from the third dimension into the second in order to move into the fourth and escape a tension or danger, a physical (or emotional) catastrophe on the third. You may do this instinctively. However, it is best for you to do this as aware, as consciously as you can.

ADVENTURES IN CHANGES, TRANSITIONS, AND DEATHS

If you find yourself in darkness, again wait just a moment. Remember that a magnificent stream of glistening light will likely soon wash through the dark flatness. Ride this light. When you feel the sensation of air or something like air, rush into your lungs or something like lungs, you will realize with relief that you are not really dead. Instead of dying, you have just traveled across dimensions of your self, of your consciousness, of your own reality which you can define for yourself.

Welcome home.

You have survived change, transition, and death.

TIME OR DIMENSIONAL TRAVEL

You may have had the brief sensation of having become a reflection, just a flat reflection of your three dimensional self. Becoming flat, two dimensional, is one way to move into the fourth dimension, the fourth dimension of the self, where time travel is the typical form of motion, the way travel around town or around the planet is typical three dimensional travel.

We can say that the third dimension, the material plane, is located in the middle of all the dimensions of reality. If you want to move up a dimension, to move around in time, either backward or forward, first you have to move your energy down a dimension. This creates a spring board effect.

When you do this, you can maybe even return from your expansion or time travel back to the third dimension with your body intact and even with the clothes you had on when you left. After all, you never left your body, did you? Maybe you never even changed your clothes while thinking through this process. You may have just been here reading or hearing – or if this is the future, remembering -- these words on these pages – right? You just traveled in your mind or your consciousness as your SELF.

ADVENTURES IN CHANGES, TRANSITIONS, AND DEATHS

Yes, so long as your biological body is still alive, you can do this return. That is, if you choose to. As all this is taking place in your mind, you can choose to visualize any or all of this as you wish. Keep this in your mind or consciousness for later when you are actually dead, as you can return to life, although maybe not to your biological body or the clothes it was wearing. You won't need those out there. You can travel as naked as you like.

Or, if you do still have a biological body, then while you are out there, seeing your SELF as out of your biological body, you can perhaps alter your physical condition by working on your energy arrangements from a higher less physical dimension of your SELF. Later, after doing this work, you can go back into your bio-body by choosing to see yourself as becoming again more dense, more physical.

Again, imagination and visualization can be quite useful here. This raising of one's energy – of one's sense of self -- to a higher frequency, a less dense form, can allow for rearrangements, restructurings, and healings that can then be moved back down to the physical plane. (Refer to the de-somatizing and re-somatizing definitions and discussions in other books in this series such as Volumes 3, 4, 11, and 14.)

THINK IN TERMS OF
DIMENSIONS OF NON-PHYSICAL ENERGY

As you master the use of your energy, and raise the power of your personal consciousness, you will have more ability to ever more consciously navigate your minor and major changes, transitions, and deaths. And, what it means for you to ever more consciously navigate will become ever more clear to you.

Gaining increasing understanding and mastery of the dying process -- or of any transitional passage -- makes life all the more worth living. In fact, the more change, transition, and death processes are mastered, the more life can be ever more fully lived.

ADVENTURES IN CHANGES, TRANSITIONS, AND DEATHS

<u>9</u>
Conceiving Of Personal Dimensions

This chapter builds on a brief look at basic traditional concepts of dimension, such as first dimension, second dimension, and so on, to both: provide a sense of what imagined or visualized non-physical travel BEYOND could look like in the mind; and, also to distinguish traditional discussions of dimension from this book's discussion of dimensions of SELF.

The *personal realm* this book refers to is the space where what this book terms one's *personal consciousness* has the option to ever more consciously move through -- to survive changes, transitions, and deaths. Having a sense of one's own personal dimensions can be valuable as you move through, as much is taking place in the non-verbal, deeper levels of the mind-brain and SELF.

PRIMER FOR LIFE'S MINOR AND MAJOR CHALLENGES AND PASSAGES

First, take a moment to think through some dimensional definition basics from the standpoint of one's personal experience of dimensions of the SELF. Here, let's build on some basics to think of personal expansion….

The following discussion and illustration of dimensions is in essence a framed diagram across several pages. Here, the content of this diagram will be lines, points, and words in italics.

FIRST NOTES ON DIMENSIONS

First there is the dimensionless point, the zero dimension:

•

Then this point, when extended, forms a line, a row of points:

•••••••••

This line or row of points represents the first dimension, as it has only one dimension, length.

⟵⟶

ADVENTURES IN CHANGES, TRANSITIONS, AND DEATHS

When you drag that line, you have a row of lines, or a plane:

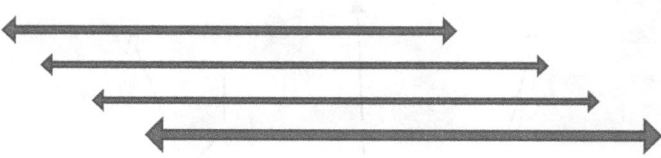

This row of lines forms this two dimensional plane:

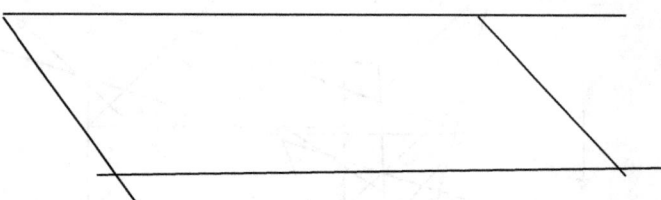

This plane (above) is the second dimension, as this has these two dimensions, length and width.

Now, when you drag this plane through space, you get something with depth as well as length and width. This is thus three dimensional reality, which you may believe know quite well:

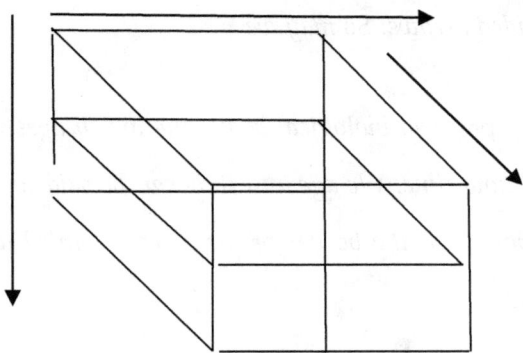

PRIMER FOR LIFE'S MINOR AND MAJOR CHALLENGES AND PASSAGES

Now, let's add a few arrows to the above diagram:

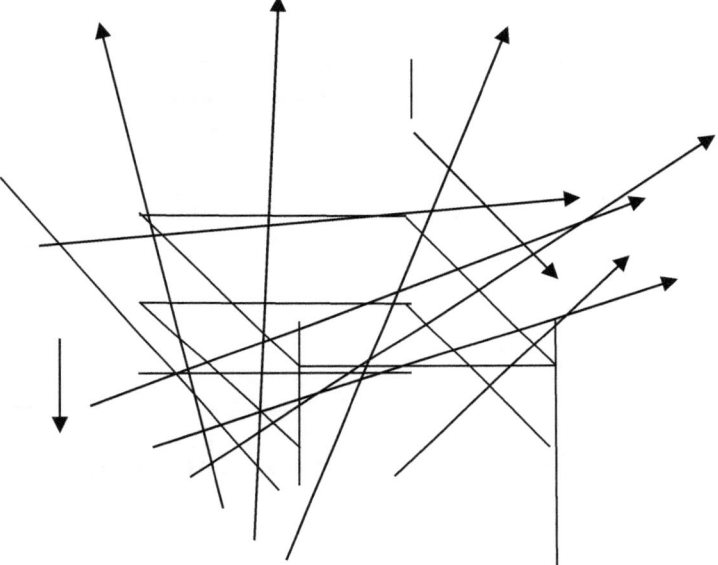

These added arrows moving in so many directions (above) suggest that we are living in more than only a physical plane 3-D reality. For example, time may be moving along one or more of these added arrows. So may we.

Living in a physical biological body, one which ages over time, you may know time. We age and thus can be said to physically exist primarily on the border of the so-called third and fourth dimensions.

ADVENTURES IN CHANGES, TRANSITIONS, AND DEATHS

A three dimensional life form moving through time can be said to be, to some degree, traveling in the fourth dimension. However, the agility of that life form's travel is a bit hampered by its ties to its third dimensional structure, the physical body in which it lives. So we are hampered, while in physical bodies, in bodies that are 3-D yet moving through time:

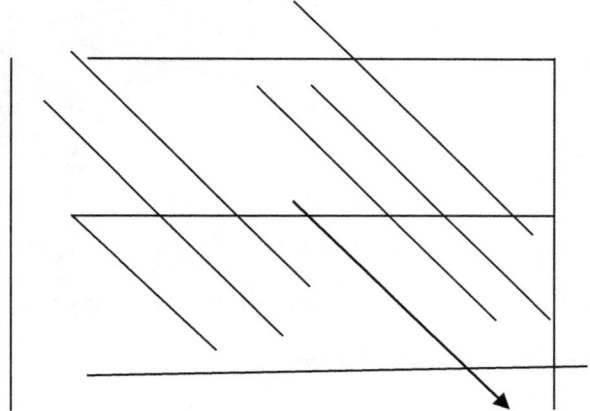

Of course, if we move that physical form rapidly enough, it transforms to something far less physically structured in a 3-D sense, and less physically dense. . . .

PRIMER FOR LIFE'S MINOR AND MAJOR CHALLENGES AND PASSAGES

Here, let's just say that the sides come off of the 3-D cube as the cube transforms to something else, a new moving or expanding shape, a new non-3-D seemingly non-geometric pattern or matrix:

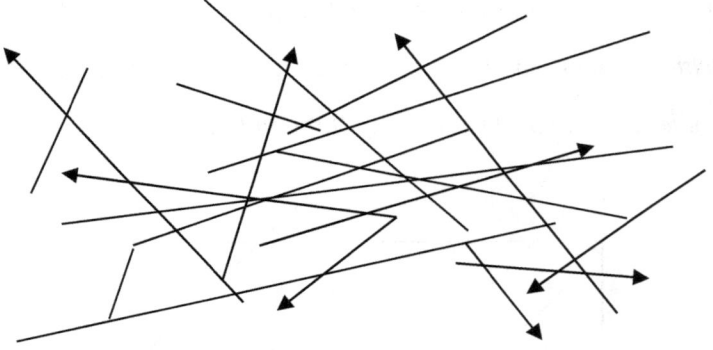

The dimensions beyond your material dimension of reality may, in a sense, progress geometrically just as do the point, the line, the plane, and the three dimensional object.

We sense ourselves reaching into the idea, the conceptual space, of our non-physical reality. Yet, it is difficult for many of us to see the progression beyond the dimension or condition of reality we think we know best, which here tends to be three dimensional (3-D) reality, and its physical plane-defined geometry.

ADVENTURES IN CHANGES, TRANSITIONS, AND DEATHS

THE LEAP

Moving the three dimensional object through time and space in all conceptual directions and dimensions, you may have what we can call here a *time burst expansion*. We can also call this time burst expansion a *LEAP*. (See detailed definition of this LEAP --this light-energy-action-process – defined in other books in this KEYS TO CONSCIOUSNESS AND SURVIVAL SERIES, such as in the HOW TO DIE AND SURVIVE books, Volumes 4, 11, and 14 of this series, and in UNVEILING THE HIDDEN INSTINCT, Volume 3 of this series.)

This LEAP is an idea, a concept, a state of mind, and is movement from one dimension of the SELF to the next. This is the sense of a *shift in state of mind and consciousness* which is usually best and most efficiently brought about when consciously constructed. This LEAP is, of course, a sort of *pattern shift* or form of *pattern death*. Each shift in dimension of self or in one's reality is in essence the move BEYOND – is the release of previous patterns as in pattern death in order to move BEYOND.

The more trained the transitioning or dying being is, the clearer and more effective the death LEAP. (Again, as noted above, refer to other books in this series for detailed discussion and definition of this LEAP and its processes.)

THE NATURE OF THE MENTAL SHIFT

Now, take that time burst or expansion referred to on previous pages, and raise it yet another level. Do not think too much about this. Just let your mind *review the nature of the mental shift* which is needed to go from: the idea of a point to the idea of a line or a straight piece of thread; from the idea of a line to the idea of a plane or a flat piece of paper; from the idea of a plane to the idea of a cube or any 3-D object; from the idea of a 3-D object to the idea of that object or body expanding or bursting out in all directions in a rapid evaporation OR EXPANSION of itself, of THE SELF.

ADVENTURES IN CHANGES, TRANSITIONS, AND DEATHS

Now, with the understanding of the mental shift it takes to think about the movement of the mind, of the awareness of the SELF, from one dimension of itself to another, you can begin to fathom a much higher dimension of this same self, of your own SELF. You can, in your mind's eye, take your *rapidly EXPANDING essence* and move it to a *place beyond motion* as you know it, where everything is present and abundant at every moment, where light streams may appear to be slow rivers beneath you.

IMAGINE, VISUALIZE, YOUR OWN BEYOND

This is perhaps the idea of your own personal BEYOND, of your own personal perhaps wondrous expanding dimension of SELF. Here you can indeed visualize light moving in and out of time, forming and unforming, appearing and disappearing, slowing down and speeding up, moving in and out of lower and higher dimensions of SELF.

This is the idea of YOU – of your *personal matrix*, of your personal energy moving. These light waves are rivers of energy running through realities. You can indeed learn to further visualize, further see, as you map your reality, again allowing your imagination to develop areas of your awareness that are further sensitizing. **Remember, this is a space, a reality, you are designing for your SELF, as this is your own personal domain.**

STAY CONSCIOUS

The death process, when it entails leaving the physical body, can cast a person unaware into this seeming non-physical space or dimension that is not defined by traditional laws of physical plane physics. To stay conscious and navigate your journey for yourself, briefly separate yourself from any overwhelming amazement at the beauty you may find there. If and when you may imagine, visualize, entire gigantic galaxies and tiny subatomic particles, all at the same time, unaided by telescope or

ADVENTURES IN CHANGES, TRANSITIONS, AND DEATHS

microscope, just seen by your mind's eye, stay focused on your actual SELF.

Remember: You can choose not to die. Your SELF can survive. You can hold your SELF together, maintain your internal cohesion rather than dissipate, rather than allow your own personal consciousness to cease existing, as your survival is your option and your right. (See the detailed definition and discussion of this *personal cohesion*, and the *cohesion exercises*, in Volume 3 of this series, UNVEILING THE HIDDEN INSTINCT. Also see related definitions and exercises in Volume 7 in this series, KEYS TO ACCESSING THE BEYOND.)

The magnificence you see or sense can be overwhelming if you forget that you are still there, still here, still surviving as your SELF. (For exercises on maintaining your own focus and center during profound changes and transitions, again see the exercises in Volume 3 of this series, UNVEILING THE HIDDERN INSTINCT, and also those

additional exercises in Volume 7 of this series, KEYS TO ACCESSING THE BEYOND.)

YOUR ENERGY MOVING
MAY FEEL TO BE EXHILARATION

You can stay centered, stay focused, stay aware, as you consciously move your SELF who is consciously surviving forward into this place BEYOND. The surprise of such perception may invite you to dissolve your focus, your own sense of SELF. But wait. Instead do hold steady, do continue to survive as your own SELF here. The Oneness can wait.

At this point, choose to hold your SELF together, to survive. Stay focused, stay conscious. Later, if you do consciously choose to dissolve, to die as a personal self, you can make this a clear and conscious choice. Later, much later.

For now, while you are choosing to continue to survive, notice your sensations. Be aware of details. Note

ADVENTURES IN CHANGES, TRANSITIONS, AND DEATHS

that, of course, once out of your biological body, you will be aware that you have no biological body, yet you will nevertheless feel your life force and any excitations of it. You begin to realize you are still alive. The divine exhilaration, the ecstasy, you may sense you feel is perhaps like being wildly in love, but millions of times more intense. If you do stay conscious here and consciously choose not to dissolve, not to die the final death and join the Oneness, you will feel with absolute certainty that you are here as YOU, that *you are surviving the great transition you are undergoing*.

A NOTE HERE:
IF YOU LATER CHOOSE TO DISSOLVE,
TO ACTUALLY DIE

The consideration of the *dimensions of self* this book offers does of course raise the question: Is there a place along this *continuum of dimensions*, along this *continuum of SELF* both here in physicality and beyond in non-physicality, where the SELF may cease to exist, can actually die? (See again Volume 3 in this series, UNVEILING THE HIDDEN INSTINCT, where the matter and finality of some mental death is discussed. See also the *Continuum of SELF* defined in Volume 10 in this series, SEEING BEYOND OUR LINE OF SIGHT.)

Certainly, the final dissolution of the self, of your self, is a possibility and an option. There may indeed be a point where surrendering to a greater presence, a Oneness, is what is chosen.

However, here is the point: Many of us have not been told that we can choose to survive even this profound transition. We can train ourselves to retain our consciousness throughout our minor and major change, transition, and dying processes. This will allow us to consciously choose whether, and if so when, we are going to die as an individual personal consciousness. The idea that we can continue to survive in the realm of our own personal consciousness is yes, just an idea; however, this is also an

ADVENTURES IN CHANGES, TRANSITIONS, AND DEATHS

idea that we can develop for ourselves. We have the option to develop this survival option, which is …

THE OPTION TO SURVIVE.

As is detailed in depth in other books in this KEYS TO CONSCIOUSNESS AND SURVIVAL SERIES, taking control of our own evolution is possible, and is our right. Where we may or may not have a fully developed non-physical realm to enter once we leave our physical biological bodies, we can start now to develop this realm, this place where we can survive: our own personal kingdom of our own personal consciousness.

We humans can choose to evolve our species into (or back into) the *inter-dimensionally mobile life forms* that we truly are. (For discussion of our survival BEYOND, and of taking control of our own evolution here and BEYOND, see: Volumes 4, 11, and 14 in this series, the HOW TO DIE AND SURVIVE books; also see the OVERRIDING THE

EXTINCTION SCENARIO books, Volumes 5 and 6 in this series; also see Volume 3 in this series, UNVEILING THE HIDDEN INSTINCT: UNDERSTANDING OUR INTERDIMENSIONAL SURVIVAL AWARENESS; also see Volume 7 in this series, KEYS TO ACCESSING THE BEYOND.)

So, if you do eventually choose to dissolve, you will perhaps move to a Oneness or a Heaven, or to another domain you define and discover. Some of this development may reflect the training you receive while living as a biological human, such as religion or philosophy, or perhaps even the *consciousness technology* you find in this KEYS TO CONSCIOUSNESS AND SURVIVAL book series. However, what is there for you may reflect what you have formed for yourself within the domain of your own personal consciousness.

Whatever this may be for you, only if you consciously choose to personally dissolve and fully enter the Oneness, can you have a say in your decision. If you are pulled in or

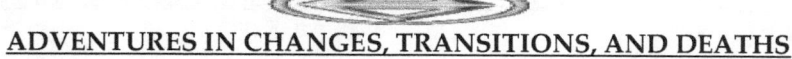

ADVENTURES IN CHANGES, TRANSITIONS, AND DEATHS

otherwise compelled to surrender your SELF and your existence to some other energy formation, then you are not being given a choice.

THIS ONE-NESS

This Oneness is likely always present, and an energy you can always be aware of. As such, you might want to ask: Would a benign Oneness demand you surrender your existence to it? Would a benign Oneness give you no say in the matter?

Other books in this series have discussed elements of the realms you may enter when leaving your physical biological body, elements that you may want to be aware of. (See for example, Volume 9, NAVIGATING LIFE'S STUFF, BOOK TWO.) First, there may appear to be trick windows, pockets, soul-traps which look and feel like the Oneness, and which may not be the Oneness or entry to the Oneness. Conscious souls who have been informed regarding what to

look for can avoid these trick windows, can detect the openings that may deceptively lead into them, and can navigate the way out should such a trap be entered.

Many traps are easy paradoxes to escape. We may learn this while living our daily lives. However, some traps lock us in far more than we expect. We may also learn this while living our daily lives.

Some traps are still more dangerous, like high security prisons where the patterns are guarded and rigid, working to defy escape. These may be beyond our usual ability to detect their nature. (In some spaces, those who enter such a lock-in trap may even risk perpetual enslavement and risk being reborn into a genetically programmed life form which uses its energy, unbeknownst to itself, in service to a cosmic hierarchy of energy domination.)

Stay aware to stay free.
Stay aware to survive both here and BEYOND.

ADVENTURES IN CHANGES, TRANSITIONS, AND DEATHS

THE GOAL IS TO STAY AWARE

This book, ADVENTURES IN CHANGES, TRANSITIONS, AND DEATHS, offers ideas and concepts for surviving -- for sustaining oneself through the challenges of living and dying. Where ever you are in your in-life, seeming end-of-life, and perhaps even after-life processes, you have the option of choosing to focus and to sustain your existence as your SELF.

You can choose to stay as aware as possible right through all your in-life, end-of-life, and perhaps even after-life transitions and dyings. If you realize that you have been enslaved as a pattern-addictable life form -- a self-programming entity -- free yourself. However, first find one or many in-life transitions, pattern deaths, to live through.

Don't just go ahead and die a biological death yet. Don't just shed your biological body and quit. Physical shedding, without proper training, training which requires

much study to absorb, may not provide you the opportunity to master the de-programming of the self – the survival of the actual SELF -- the mastery each and every one of us has a right to.

The ultimate dimension of you is you.

ADVENTURES IN CHANGES, TRANSITIONS, AND DEATHS

10
Shedding Your Skin

> *We can find ourselves ready to change, to undergo a transition, to let some pattern that has been part of us go. Somehow we begin to feel our skin is not fitting us any longer. There are times when we can sense this and yet not consciously know this. When it comes time to shed this skin, when we do in some way sense this, we may not be ready to or want to understand this. This chapter explores the concept of shedding as a part of the process of change, transition, and death.*

Each and every one of us reaches a point in life, usually several times, when some part of our particular way of seeing the world, of behaving, of relating, of being -- when some bit of our particular identity or reality -- no longer seems to fit us, or be good for us, or be right for us, or at least no longer entirely fits, or is entirely good, or is entirely right. We may feel as if we have outgrown

something ... perhaps that we are wearing shoes that are now too small....

ALL TRANSITIONS AND DEATHS ARE A SHEDDING

We have talked about the importance of spotting windows of opportunity, and, even before that, of knowing when we are at forks in our roads. (See again Chapters 5 and 6.) Usually, prior to coming to a fork in the road, or to a window of opportunity, we have at least the vague sense of the need for shedding or for moving through a window of opportunity.

However, we frequently are not aware of what the sensations we are experiencing are telling us, and thus do not detect windows of opportunity or forks in our paths until we are either already deep into them or miss them.

As with detecting forks and windows, we tend to miss seeing that we need to shed our skins until we are either deep into the process, completed with the process, or well

ADVENTURES IN CHANGES, TRANSITIONS, AND DEATHS

into a much later shedding. Or, we entirely miss our sheddings, not realizing that these have taken place, which results in our not using them well or not bringing them to healthy completion.

Or, we simply get stuck in a holding pattern (a paradox) while resisting the shedding of even that holding pattern, that paradox, itself. (Of course, we do want to ask whether we ourselves are doing the resisting, or the pattern itself is doing the resisting. For in depth discussion of this matter, see the book by this author titled, SEEING THE HIDDEN FACE OF ADDICTION: DETECTING AND CONFRONTING THIS INVASIVE PRESENCE.)

Still, shedding is as much a part of change and transition in both life and death as is any other function. You shed skin cells and hair every day. If you are an adult, you have, most likely, already shed several relationships and behaviors.

PRIMER FOR LIFE'S MINOR AND MAJOR CHALLENGES AND PASSAGES

People who die physical deaths shed their biological bodies. Basically, most of our physical deaths take place when we have outgrown or over-damaged our bodies. Our bodies are then no longer our vehicles.

The same is true of our relationships, our jobs, our addictions, and any of our behaviors. There can come a time for shedding some part or all of certain patterns.

Some sheddings are complete cut-offs, endings, abrupt deaths. And, other sheddings are more subtle perhaps. These may be transitions, transformations, and transcendences of the sometimes less visible patterns and sub-patterns that may be there within situations, behaviors, relationships, states of mind, and so on.

HOW YOU KNOW YOUR SKIN'S TOO TIGHT

Yes, too often the pressure to shed sneaks up on us. We finally notice that the skin of a situation, or of a behavior, or of a relationship, or of a body -- or maybe even of a life

ADVENTURES IN CHANGES, TRANSITIONS, AND DEATHS

itself, is far too tight -- that we have outgrown it the way a snake outgrows its skin.

You can get more out of the shedding process by recognizing whether and when you are at its threshold. How do you do this? Become very alert to subtleties:

- Notice shifts in your ability to concentrate.

- Notice changes in your enthusiasm.

- Notice when you feel claustrophobic or trapped -- physically, emotionally, intellectually, spiritually.

- Notice if you are regularly exhibiting troubled behavior (which is detrimental to yourself or others).

- Notice to what degree you function on automatic, generally mindlessly.

- Notice how you respond when you stop for a moment's reflection and ask yourself, "Who am I and why am I here?"

If you find that your life takes on less and less meaning for you – that you are less and less invested in the meaning of your life -- pay attention. Do not assume that while physical survival is essential here in the physical plane where we live in our biological bodies, physical survival alone brings all meaning available. It may and it may not, depending upon the effect upon you of your achieving this survival.

What might you want to re-frame? What part of your process might you be able to see differently?

Are you struggling in some way? Is this a struggle for survival, or a struggle for the survival of an old pattern that must go? Is a problem pattern pulling and even draining your personal resources away from you – away from your own survival?

ADVENTURES IN CHANGES, TRANSITIONS, AND DEATHS

GETTING OUT

You know when it is time to shed your skin, or the skin of some piece of your patterning. You may feel caged in, boxed in, trapped, by some of the patterns and or sub-patterns in your life. You may feel you are losing your SELF and your free will to the demands of problem patterns that do not serve you well, that your problem patterns are taking over. Pay attention. What may appear to be about your own survival may be the drive of a problem pattern to survive at your own expense

As you see more and more about what is happening here, your actual SELF can move BEYOND problem patterns to work toward the survival of your actual SELF -- not that patterns that have been dominating it.

Once you allow yourself to see the truth, to detect the need for shedding, you may be ready to let yourself out of the part of your situation or pattern that must go -- out of

that particular pattern's skin. Here's where there is, sometimes, a strong resistance. Either you or the people around you may not want you to change. (And again, we can ask whether it is actually the patterns you carry that do not want you to change.)

Get to know what the need for shedding feels like. Open your eyes to the forks in the road and the windows of opportunity for change that are appearing. Once you know what to look for, if there are indeed reasons to be shedding, these are everywhere.

TAKES STEPS TO PLAN
THE TRANSITION AND CHANGE EXPERIENCE

Then, take steps to understand what it is that you want to shed, how this might be shed, how this process will be navigated and experienced. Plan the states of mind you may experience during the lead up to shedding, and then during the shedding process itself, and also following the shedding process, following the death of the body of behavior you have outgrown.

ADVENTURES IN CHANGES, TRANSITIONS, AND DEATHS

You can make changes for the better. Do not let anyone tell you that you cannot get there from here. This statement reveals our deep programming to believe in severe limitations. When it comes to your own sense of SELF, your own perception of who you are, well then, you can move your idea of your SELF anywhere you want from here. You just need a map and a vehicle, and some sense of direction....

WHY SOME PEOPLE PREFER PHYSICAL DEATH

When you are without the map and the vehicle of change, or have not yet found the courage to read the map and drive the vehicle, you may stay quite stuck. You know the stuck, trapped, no exit feeling: It's that phase called "paradox" described in Chapters 5 and 6.

Some persons remain entirely or substantially trapped within a paradox -- the same, repeating, or similar sort of paradox -- for most of their lives. When the pressure

to shed becomes unbearably great, they may either break down, grow very reckless, do something extreme, become ever more addicted to something unhealthy and unsafe, or perhaps get sick and die or suicide and die.

Or, the pressure can be the inspiration to make the change to save the life of the SELF – and to not save the problem patterning that is harming or killing the SELF.

While actions such as breaking down, doing something extreme, or perhaps getting sick and dying, or suiciding, are truly unfortunate, traumatic, and sad developments, they are, ironically, when stumbled into unintentionally, easy ways out. <u>Do not misunderstand this comment</u>. Not all physical illness, and terminal disease, and not all suicide is the result of a long-term personal resistance to the shedding of paradox. A significant portion of illness and even of suicide is the expression of overarching global conditions which are too large for those who are untrained to see.

ADVENTURES IN CHANGES, TRANSITIONS, AND DEATHS

EFFECTS OF RESISTANCE TO SHEDDING

Still, some persons are trapped for a long long time and remain resistant to dying the living death of the pattern which traps them. They may see no exit, no way to shed their skins except physical death. And then, on some level, they decide to get out this way. Because the decision is usually an unconscious one, it does not seem to be a decision. Instead it is seen as an unfortunate event.

One of the most unfortunate developments is the moving of a troubled behavior pattern from the psychological to the physical realm. This allows trapped energy to become more dense, more physical. It is not surprising that many psychological and spiritual disturbances take on explicit physical and behavioral aspects such as drug addiction, sex addiction, domestic violence, accident-prone-ness, and, of course, physical pain and illness.

Beings who live in the material plane, as you do, pull whatever they can into a place where they can see it. There is a drive to "make real" energies which are perceived but not seen.

This drive is valuable when it calls attention to energy disturbances and implicit patterns that might not otherwise be seen. Yet, at the same time, this "physicalizing" or "somaticization" (pronounced: so-mah-tih-ciz-aye-shun) of a hidden condition can result in physical suffering without any healing or even any recognition of the condition from which it stems. Basically, you can make yourself sick pulling the energy in to physical form unless you are trained to work with it.

It is best to <u>*de*-structure and shed</u> detrimental patterns before they become physicalized or more physicalized. This means that one must be highly conscious of these patterns long before they make themselves visible to the physical eye. Much more is accomplished when the work is done above the level of the physical body and plane. Surgery on

ADVENTURES IN CHANGES, TRANSITIONS, AND DEATHS

energy patterns is possible and essential. (Other volumes in this series discuss this treatment, such as the discussion on de-somatizing in Volume 3, UNVEILING THE HIDDEN INSTINCT.)

THE RIGHT TO DIE

The above is quite true. Still, even physical death can be a great teacher and releaser.

This is not to advocate for the unconscious stumbling into terminal disease or impulsive or irresponsible suicide. However, this is also not an argument against conscious, highly informed and highly responsible physical death as a respectable way out of the skin of a life that one has outgrown.

The right to die both as pain free and as consciously as possible must be defended. The art and science of conscious change, transition, and death, even of body exit itself, must be taught.

We already do know much more about *body exit* and *self-deliverance* than we realize. (See definitions of and exercises regarding body exit and self deliverance in the HOW TO DIE AND SURVIVE BOOKS, Volumes 4, 11, and 14 in this KEYS TO CONSCIOUSNESS AND SURVIVAL SERIES.) Certainly, there are persons who give advice regarding medicinal and mechanical means of dying. However, there are many ways of detaching from a pattern or even from the body itself that require no assistance. These techniques are best learned and practiced while living one's daily life in one's biological body. These techniques are presented in other books in this KEYS TO CONSCIOUSNESS AND SURVIVAL SERIES (such as the above-noted Volumes, 4, 11, and 14, the HOW TO DIE AND SURVIVE books.) You have a right to this information, but only with the moral commitment to use it right.

11
Harvesting Your Transition And Death Processes

Whether you are dying a death of a behavior or dying a physical death, you must take responsibility for the energy you release when old patterns die. The harvest is yours.

Stay conscious of this. Do not sell or trade your product, the arrangement of energy you have cultivated, at the market unless the exchange is toward an ever more right use and freedom of will.

Once you begin to make more and more your own the concepts that your major transitions are all deaths, and that you can master each and every one of your death processes, you can gain ever more power over the course of your life and of your evolution. As you grow in this understanding, you can gain an increasing say in the use of the energy you have cultivated and arranged in your life.

At any moment you choose, you can more and more sense, increasingly access, the energy flowing through you and through any dimension of your own personal reality.

You help cultivate and arrange this energy, forming your own *personal energy matrix*, your own identity, the SELF who can learn to survive here and BEYOND. You release your energy into your reality. (Again see Volume 3, UNVEILING THE HIDDEN INSTINCT, for definitions and exercises regarding your energy matrix.)

Energy is a convenient word here, although this energy is more a concept, one not tied to physical plane definitions and restrictions. In this sense, you have as much right to your own energy as anyone or anything else does. You have as much right to your own energy so long as you use it to fuel the right and honorable use of will.

Do stay aware. You can feel when you or others (or patterns themselves) may be drawing upon your energy for other than the right and honorable use of will.

ADVENTURES IN CHANGES, TRANSITIONS, AND DEATHS

TRANSITION AND DEATH AS A GIFT

Do not fear change. Change itself need not be the issue. And fear itself, well fear is more than simply a word. Fear is a label for many different emotions and sensations. Understand the sensations of what gets called fear. See our programming to experience both useful and harmful or dangerous fear, both the protective awareness and the blinding fear defined in Chapter 2.

Fear congests and weakens your energy. Remember that there is, throughout the cosmos, a perpetual flow of change, in which forces are *always* interweaving and disentangling, contracting and expanding. This is called samsura or incessant motion by Buddhists. Some of this motion is smooth. Some of it is rocky, and some of it is convulsive. But all of it is change. Change is incessant.

And so, when a change feels in any way like a death, look closely. Could the death sensation be about a pattern

that needs to be dying? Could this pattern death or change be an opportunity? A gift? Change is, after all, the freeing of energy.

**DYNAMICS OF PERSONAL
INTER-DIMENSIONAL CHANGE**

Resistance to change can be stagnation. A long term paradox pattern can become a stagnation of energy. Too many elect, of what they believe to be their own free wills, to stagnate, to go against the flow, to resist change. All too often, it is the problem pattern resisting change, seeking not to die. It is the problem pattern holding you stuck in the trap of a rigid no-exit paradox – not you your SELF. The problem pattern is seeking to survive at your expense.

This is not surprising. We have not allowed ourselves -- or have not been allowed -- to fully understand the dynamics of what is ultimately inter-dimensional change. We are held in a rather unenlightened state, because we are more easily controlled there -- controlled by our own problem patterns (and patterns of addiction to our problem

ADVENTURES IN CHANGES, TRANSITIONS, AND DEATHS

patterns), and also by our own social and political systems, and by other forces too large for us to see.

We unenlightened may tend to resist change, perhaps feeling change to be disconcerting or threatening, and death as the end rather than as a shift into a new dimension of SELF. The enlightened person need not resist the flow of the life force throughout the dimensions, rather opens to a recognition of this flow and to a movement *with* this flow.

BE EVER MORE CONSCIOUS
OF FORCES AND FACTORS HERE AND BEYOND

The greater one's understanding of this most dynamic and divine order, the more one's actions will harmonize with it. At the same time, such a greater and more conscious understanding will also prevent the kidnapping of your energy by forces and factors not really here for your own good.

Just as there are predators in the jungle, there may be predatory forces present in non-physical dimensions, forces and presences that seek to use your energy arrangements and transitions and releases for their own purposes.

Keep in mind that a problem pattern that is draining you – that is working to survive at your expense – is itself a predator.

PREPARING FOR THE HARVEST

We have touched on the notion that your energy patterning is yours. Because you produce your arrangement of your energy, moving it into healthy and unhealthy patterns, and because you release pieces or all of your arrangement of your energy when you change or die, you are responsible for what your energy does and where it goes.

This means that you, as a responsible being, must always be learning more about mastering the flow of your

ADVENTURES IN CHANGES, TRANSITIONS, AND DEATHS

energy in and out of patterns and life transitions and dimensions of your reality. You must be as conscious as possible of the phases of transition and transcendence. You must be ever alert for indication of sheddings, forks, and windows. You must stay as conscious as you can through all your changes, transitions, and deaths -- physical and non-physical, in order to be certain you do not surrender, sign over, or land your energy in a place where you lose say, lose free will, over its use.

It is your responsibility then to prepare for the appropriate and conscious harvest of your energy which takes place during and following each and every one of your minor and major changes, transitions, and dying processes.

To best prepare for your harvest, take control of your life. Although you cannot control all the events around you, you can direct, navigate, your ride through them.

PRIMER FOR LIFE'S MINOR AND MAJOR CHALLENGES AND PASSAGES

- Become sensitive to the phases, sheddings, forks, and windows we have discussed.

- During any difficult transition, stay focused on a high point within what you feel is your physical body, or a metaphor for a physical body. It is best to select either the area in the center of the forehead or at the top of the head to stay connected to.

- Hold on to this connection, keep returning to the idea of it, as if there were a cord attached to it. To survive at this juncture in your process, stay connected this way. (And always, now or later in your process, know to stay connected with your SELF.)

- If you want to let go of the cord, the connection from your biological body to your SELF, you may. However, try to do so quite consciously, as if you are knowingly releasing the reigns while riding a wild horse. Check the terrain out beforehand. Are there any traps or trick windows leading to dead ends or

ADVENTURES IN CHANGES, TRANSITIONS, AND DEATHS

undesirable nests for your energy? These must be avoided. Can you see clearly what is calling you and coming at you? Other books in this series detail the various releases of the cord that you might undertake at this juncture. For now, letting go, yet being conscious as you do, is enough of a description. (For definitions, details, and exercises regarding identifying and releasing cords, refer to Volume 4 in this series, HOW TO DIE AND SURVIVE, BOOK ONE.)

- You do have the right to choose to fully die, to fully cease to exist on all levels. However, before you elect this form of full and final release, do so knowing that you are freeing your energy for absorption by your environment in time, in space, in the cosmos. The harvest will no longer be specifically yours then.

- To fully die, to fully release, to turn over your harvest to some other force or factor or presence, first learn more about the release of energy brought about by your dying process.

- Always remember that you do have the right **_NOT to die_**, the right to survive as your SELF.

- Of course, choosing to fully die, to entirely cease to exist, is also your right – when you are making a fully informed and fully responsible decision. So, this full release, this full and final death, may not be a detrimental choice, so long as you know well what you are doing, know well how final this will be, and know well where you are sending or releasing your energy.

- It is your responsibility to keep your eyes -- your sensory mechanisms -- open and notice what systems are there to receive – to absorb, to swallow your energy. Many times those forces and factors lure beings in to full surrender for their own purposes and agendas – not to serve you.

ADVENTURES IN CHANGES, TRANSITIONS, AND DEATHS

- Whether you are dying a death of a behavior or dying a physical death, you must take responsibility for the energy you release when old patterns die. The harvest is yours. Stay conscious of this. Do not sell or trade your product, the arrangement of energy you have cultivated, at the market unless the exchange is toward an ever more right use and freedom of will. If you feel unprepared to make such an assessment, keep your energy under your wing and continue to evolve it.

- You have a right to choose for your SELF whether to die and cease to exist, or to …

die and survive.

PRIMER FOR LIFE'S MINOR AND MAJOR CHALLENGES AND PASSAGES

ADVENTURES IN CHANGES, TRANSITIONS, AND DEATHS

12
From Personal Apocalypse Into Power

This chapter looks at the overall sense that we can move from low points, even states of fear and or protective awareness – that we can mobilize ourselves, the mind, awareness, and spirit. There is ever more power to be discovered in ourselves. There is so much there for us to discover, to access, to release to ourselves. There is also so much power locked up in the patterns we have established and or are caught in, which is also power that can be released by us to us.

As a human in a physical biological body, you know what ordeals can be faced by life forms living in the third dimension. These ordeals can encourage your spiritual growth. They can also distract you from spiritual growth.

The journey through your human incarnation is superbly challenging. And the potential for what is called "the quickening of the soul" is profoundly immense during your human incarnation.

Try to remember this in your living moments of stress and even distress, or even anguish. And try to receive this message in its entirety at the hour of your physical death.

THE DENIAL OF MORE

As a biological human in a biological body, it may be easy for you to think that there exists nothing but this third dimension physical plane reality– that there is only material reality and nothing else – and, therefore, that all life forms have biological bodies and only those. Although a human often begins to feel that there might be more to her or his reality than meets the physical eye, for many the general assumption remains that nothing living can really exist without a three dimensional, 3-D, body. (Many times, even when religion offers concepts of more than just the life here

ADVENTURES IN CHANGES, TRANSITIONS, AND DEATHS

on Earth, people's minds hang on to the physical reality as the reality they see so therefore believe in on a day to day basis. The old seeing is believing view is central.)

Coming to the sense, the realization that we exist along a continuum from physicality to non-physicality, is key here. (See other books in this series, such as Volume 10, SEEING BEYOND OUR LINE OF SIGHT, for definition and discussion of this inter-dimensional awareness, and of the inter-dimensional CONTINUUM we exist on.)

As the interdimensional awareness of a human being matures – evolves itself, the developing of higher, less physical plane-centered, domains of the self takes place.

As we, of the human life form, extend our awareness of our reality to include the idea of our own non-physicality, of what can be there beyond the base physical realm, we can begin to center ourselves across a wider spectrum from physical to non-physical.

As we do, our focus becomes less restricted, less primarily physical. Our sense of ourselves becomes less and less dense, more and more aware of our expansion into realms less physically dense than the physical body. Try to encourage this expansion in yourself. You will be contributing to your own and your species' evolution. Remember, this expansion is conceptual and not physical, and is:

**a state of mind,
a state of awareness,
a state of self.**

The full essence of the universe, including the realm within our own consciousness, is one which lies beyond the grasp of the existing human intellect. Fortunately, the collective human mind is beginning to progress through the development of its intellect into a new form of what we can call the inter-dimensional intelligence.

(See other books in this KEYS TO CONSCIOUSNESS AND SURVIVAL SERIES for in-depth definition and

ADVENTURES IN CHANGES, TRANSITIONS, AND DEATHS

discussion of this inter-dimensional intelligence, such as Volume 6, OVERRIDING THE EXTINCTION SCENARIO, PART TWO.)

THE IMPORTANCE OF DENSITY

A general understanding of density is essential here, both to ease the conceptual passage from physical death to the beyond, from physical to non-physical, and, while in this particular physical plane lifetime, to understand how programming and pattern addictions can be transcended. In reading the following review, remember that it helps to think in pictures in order to have an understanding of density work for you. You are, in a sense, being asked to conceptually "lighten up," to imagine you de-densify. In a less dense form, your energy is lighter, more malleable, more easily rearranged. Attempt to imagine the light described below as a river of energy.

- The less dense, the more like fluid light, that you sense (or imagine) yourself to become, the greater your sensitivity and inter-dimensional awareness will be. (Again, see other books in this series for definition and discussion of this inter-dimensional awareness.)

- The concept (and thus the imagined experience) of fluid light is not itself very dense. It has almost no density. After all, it is a just concept.

- Beings, life forms, can be viewed as taking on varying degrees of conceptual density. A life form locates along an imagined or actual continuum of most dense to least dense.

- As you expand your range of awareness, grow in consciousness, your concept of your own SELF itself becomes less dense. This can feel "ungrounding" to those unschooled in this process, as well as to those schooled in this process.

ADVENTURES IN CHANGES, TRANSITIONS, AND DEATHS

- By your expanding your awareness up the scale to include the idea of your own decreasing density, your mind and your spirit, your SELF, become less weighed down by the compactness of <u>belief</u> in physical reality as the only reality.

- As this "unweighting" takes place, the sense of the ***diminishing of your body relative to the expansion of your energy*** begins. You may feel a bit disoriented or even crazed by this sensation, as if you are "losing it," becoming "unglued." If so, you are experiencing the somewhat unsettling effects of ***de-cohesion***, diminishing cohesion. You are really feeling the effect of enhanced "entropy." (See Volume 3 in this series, UNVEILING THE HIDDEN INSTINCT, for definition and discussion of this de-cohesion and related concepts.)

- Entropy is the tendency of matter to dissipate in the process of what this book describes as de-cohesion.

As our view of matter itself becomes less dense, less compact, less cohesive, we ourselves may sense or imagine that our physical biological presences gain entropy, increasingly dissipate. Matter begins to weighs less and less per square millimeter and is thus less weighed down. The physical matter of "you" as a physical body becomes less tightly organized in a material sense (but more complex in a multi-dimensional sense).

Try not to think about all this too very much. Visualize, imagine, explore, sensitize, expand to reach BEYOND.

Misunderstanding one's conceptual consciousness realm is one of the dangers of over-intellectualizing important inter-dimensional concepts. Just allow these ideas to be with you. After a while these ideas will be comprehensible in new ways.

ADVENTURES IN CHANGES, TRANSITIONS, AND DEATHS

Third dimensional beings and objects such as we are are not the most dense. Those found in the zero, first and second -- the denser dimensions -- are far more dense and compact. Still, you are indeed quite dense, as are all physical bodies.

CONSCIOUSNESS TECHNOLOGY

Awaken your concept of your SELF, of your consciousnesses. Learning to imagine you move your being through densities is essential.

To do so, you must become increasingly adept in the *consciousness technology* **this book and this KEYS TO CONSCIOUSNESS AND SURVIVAL book series presents. This is the technology by which consciousness can become highly aware of itself and profoundly enhance its functioning, freedom, and survival.**

You, as a consciousness, are able to manifest your essence in increasing complexity and vastness throughout all the imagined and actual dimensions of your SELF. You, just as any life form, can evolve increasing degrees of awareness and consciousness.

As a biological human living on Earth, you are already part of a life system of conscious interaction -- a social system which has a government and an economy. Yet, how much freedom is available to you within the system you so-called "belong to"? And, do you really belong to that system? A higher level of consciousness *must* be achieved in order to answer this and to preserve free will as you further evolve.

REACHING THROUGH TO THE SUPERMIND

You can learn to recognize the Supermind. Untrained, your efforts may not reach you through to the Supermind. Your ignorance (which may have been programmed into you, perhaps even by predatory forces and factors) may not manage to transcend itself. So how do you, with physical

ADVENTURES IN CHANGES, TRANSITIONS, AND DEATHS

reality limitations, ascend to your rightful place in the cosmic hierarchy of energy and awareness?

Your ascendance can be actuated by the Consciousness Force, which works toward the emergence of its powers into each being's -- in this case your -- consciousness. You can allow this *super*conscience to descend into you and uplift you, to formulate the process of your transcendence and ascendance back to your rightful level of high consciousness – and yes, to your rightful SURVIVAL.

HOWEVER, YOU MUST WAIT UNTIL YOU HAVE STUDIED SUBTLE REALITIES ENOUGH TO KNOW WHEN YOU ARE IN CONTACT WITH THE TRUE SUPERCONSCIENCE AND NOT A FORCE POSING AS THE SUPERCONSCIENCE.

Otherwise, you are interacting your energy with a higher power, even surrendering your energy to a higher

PRIMER FOR LIFE'S MINOR AND MAJOR CHALLENGES AND PASSAGES

power, but not necessarily the higher power you would choose of your own free will had you enough information to do or not to do so.

This concept is important here, in that during the dying process, whether it is a living transition or a physical shedding, energy is released. As noted elsewhere in this book, this energy is sometimes released to other than one's own SELF, to other than one's own personal consciousness.

(For example, many persons recovering from explicit addictions are overwhelmed by their newly released energy and quickly give it away again. Sometimes they trap it in the same or a new pattern addiction. Sometimes, they surrender the energy to a higher power. Yet, to which higher power? And, higher than what is that power?)

You can choose to evolve your SELF without outside intervention. You can make this decision to evolve for your SELF. The elements of the higher consciousness you seek are already present within you. Accessing these and developing

ADVENTURES IN CHANGES, TRANSITIONS, AND DEATHS

these is the challenge. Decide for yourself. But decide consciously and stay conscious. The journey is yours. Travel it your way.

BELIEVING IN MORE AND FINDING IT

Most life forms see so little of what is really here. Life forms define their realities based upon the illusions they allow themselves to believe in – or are programmed to believe in. All they really see are shadows of Truth, shadows of reality. In these shadows live the illusions which hold us captive.

Turn on the light! Death is not what you may believe it to be! Nothing dies in the so-called "conventional" sense. Nothing stops moving -- matter is always in motion, whether organic or inorganic.

Examine information for truth. Humans must do this. Truth has been severely distorted by language and culture. The precious consciousness of humanity is buried within an elaborate hierarchy of distortion which veils truth. Human words and beliefs are part of this elaborate distortion. *Our programming itself underlies this elaborate distortion.*

A spiritual truth, to be honestly relayed in its wholeness, cannot be distorted. A spiritual truth, without ever being intellectualized by the brain of a human or any other life form, can coalesce itself into an experience, an awareness, an image, or a symbol. That experience, awareness, image, or symbol can again unfold in the eye of its beholder -- depending upon the sophistication of the beholder in terms of his or her readiness -- into varying degrees of truth.

Let this unfolding begin within you. When you are ready to understand the truth, YOUR TRUTH, you will recognize it as it comes to you. Again, filter what comes to you to be certain predatory forces are not moving in while disguising themselves. This is not about being paranoid. This is about having wise awareness.

ADVENTURES IN CHANGES, TRANSITIONS, AND DEATHS

POWER IS IN KNOWING WHO YOU ARE

Know who you are.

Know that every individual soul is a micro-consciousness, one which affects the macro-consciousness. Every soul vibrates at its own frequency of consciousness. This frequency can be raised -- evolved by that soul. Spiritual evolution is a constant developing of form, spiritual form. Development involves journeying through dimensions of reality. The sole purpose of any spirit coming into the third dimension of reality (such as you have on Earth) is to work toward manifesting what some will define as the indwelling spirit.

Know who and what spirit is coming into the third dimension through you. Ideally YOU are coming into the third dimension through YOU.

When free to, nature evolves in this direction: the progression is from matter extending toward mind. The

evolution of matter through time is from the lower to the higher dimensions. Every soul has the right to ascend to a higher consciousness.

Commit to this growth for the good of us all. Your great soul has the potential to advance the evolution of humanity, of other souls whether human or not, and to spread true enlightenment.

GREATNESS OF BEING

You are great soul. You are your own higher consciousness. You can bring the energy generated by a transformation of your own consciousness to the collective energy pool. You can contribute to a global, a cosmic, transformation that will help end the dictatorial cultivation, wasting, and kidnapping of your and others' physical plane energies.

Always seek authenticity in the expression of your power -- do not be fooled by the temptations of self-doubt

ADVENTURES IN CHANGES, TRANSITIONS, AND DEATHS

and negativity. In nonchalance and noncommittal, you are surrendering to enslavement, to greater problem pattern addiction, to the capturing and killing of free will! *You can help to protect free will by becoming ever more free.*

STAY CONSCIOUS

Now that we have said that there is no such thing as death, a little further elaboration on this is necessary. There is a great difference between cyclical and absolute death. When free will disappears entirely from the cosmos, this will be the absolute death of free will. Matter and energy may live on in some form, perhaps even eternally; however, the will, the free will can be permanently eliminated.

This will not be an adventure in death. This will be the end of the life of an energy force you have come to call "freedom." Do not allow this transition into an entirely mechanical, programmed, robotic, will-less, soul-less universe to happen. Stay conscious.

PRIMER FOR LIFE'S MINOR AND MAJOR CHALLENGES AND PASSAGES

ADVENTURES IN CHANGES, TRANSITIONS, AND DEATHS

EPILOGUE:
Revolution And Death

In that the ideas on these pages may press the limits of our minds and also of our societal conventions just a little, these concepts are perhaps somewhat revolutionary. Death, whatever form it may take, offers the opportunity for transcendence, but in no way guarantees it. Again it is important to die well, whether or not the death in question is biological. Change, transition, and death processes can be navigated with increasing awareness, and even increasing power, when conducted ever more consciously.

Every day, even every moment of our lives, we are in the process of small and large, minor and major, unseen and quite visible, changes, transitions, and death processes. These are taking place in our daily lives, during all parts of our lives, and also in end-of-life, and perhaps even in after-life processes.

Our lives give us great opportunities to learn about ourselves and our own personal power -- to see how consciously we can move through our changes, transitions, and deaths. We can become ever more aware of how we feel during these processes, of what the signs are that we are experiencing these processes, and of what the stages or patterns of these processes feel like.

All this prepares us for the bigger challenges we may face, for the more intense and or more profound processes, eventually even for the death and dying processes we associate with biological death itself.

Ultimately, how aware, how conscious of our experiences, sensations, and energetic or even non-physical environments we can be during the changes, transitions, and deaths we experience can determine how we make it through, even how we survive.

ADVENTURES IN CHANGES, TRANSITIONS, AND DEATHS

We can gain more connection to ourselves, to our actual SELVES who may be able to learn to exist even independent of our biology. We can grow ever more aware of ourselves as beings who are not necessarily tied to our biological bodies, who can therefore die and survive.

THEY SAY WE THINK, BUT WHO IS IT THINKING?

They say we think; therefore we are. But who are we? What thinks? The brain? The mind? Is there a difference? And what is this thing we call thinking?

Contained in a skull no larger than a deflated soccer ball and physically manifested in the form of a wrinkled blob we call *brain,* the human mind is an intractable entity. This human mind, seemingly based in the biological brain that houses it, is difficult to locate but boundaryless, capable of amazing feats but weak and fallible, seemingly autonomous and yet tending toward the convenience of supposedly survival oriented pre-programming which can

at times run awry and result in problematic, frequently undesirable, sometimes even dangerous, troubled habitual behaviors and other problem pattern addictions.

One of the toughest of all our pattern addictions is our programmed-in addiction to our reality – or to what we have been programmed to believe is our reality. Somehow, our brains are wired to demand our dependence on what is, our deep reliance on our seeming reality, and for this to be a reality check on all reality. We, our minds -- or should we say basically our brains, cling to what is, or to what we are told is, refusing to let it die unless we are pushed to the edge and lose control or fitfully relinquish it. And then there may be a difficult or even tortured transition or death process, rather than a fruitful one.

Yet, this is our programmed-in pattern addiction to a limited reality we have been programmed to believe is real. This programming we live within and by is so extensive that we do not see the all encompassing no-exit paradoxes (and paradoxes within paradoxes) en-trapping us.

ADVENTURES IN CHANGES, TRANSITIONS, AND DEATHS

WHEN THE WORLD AS WE KNOW IT DIES

When the world as we know it, the reality upon which we have become so dependent, dies, do we die too? Must we die too?

Or is it the implanted programming that must die for us to survive?

They say that we live; therefore we die. But who says this? Who lives? What dies?

Could we be prisoner of a lie? Could it be we are programmed not to know we need not die? Not to know we can survive?

THE POLITICS OF DEATH

Could death be something different than we have come to believe it to be? Can we break free of the shackles of our programming and see through our fears, our sufferings, our difficult transitions, our mental, emotional,

spiritual, and even physical deaths? Can we look through the veil of deception which humanity has allowed itself to – or has been programmed to -- live beneath? Can we reach BEYOND what we are told is who and what we are? Can we break free of our programming and see ever more about what is really happening here, and ...

SEE THE TRUTH ABOUT
OUR SURVIVAL OPTIONS HERE AND BEYOND.

YES! But first we must be willing, be daring enough, to ask:

Are we programmed to die? Why do each and every one of our cells have a genetic plan to die off after a certain number of divisions? Are we genetically programmed to die physical deaths? Are we genetically programmed to believe that we have to cease to exist when we die, that our biological death is absolutely final? And is this programmed-in belief so all powerful that it controls us, kills us, makes our deaths final? (See the in depth discussion

ADVENTURES IN CHANGES, TRANSITIONS, AND DEATHS

of these matters in Volume 6 of this series, OVERRIDING THE EXTINCTION SCENARIO, PART TWO.)

**Why have we not known with certainty that
who we are, our actual SELF,
can learn to survive changes and transitions and
eventually develop means of surviving
BEYOND biological death?
Is this because we simply do not know –
or are programmed not to know –
or are programmed not to ask –
or simply have not been told we can develop this
understanding within ourselves now.**

We must ask whether we have been brainwashed, programmed, into acceptance of the lie about our dying, about our not being able to learn to survive beyond biological death. Why would this programming of us, of our brains and minds, be happening? What force or intelligence

or energy could have focused upon our genetic coding so closely as to create such a limited reality in our minds?

WE MUST ASK

We must dare to ask: Are we biological, fleshy robots? Do we reflect a sallow mechanical light in our eyes, the light of programmed-in obedience and will-less-ness, the glow of hypnotization? Have we succumbed to a daze in modern years, or have we always been part of a very large programmed-in mindlessness -- are we biotech at its finest? Or biotech gone wrong?

If Earth is a fantastic macrocosmic laboratory and we are prisoner-subjects in a massive experiment too large for our human minds to fathom, then our learning the truth can lead to startling discoveries regarding our captors. Perhaps we can capture control of our wills and set them free.

Only a revolution in human awareness can free us. But what would this freedom look like? Would it be very

ADVENTURES IN CHANGES, TRANSITIONS, AND DEATHS

much different from the way we live and look now? Can we really be free as long as we are subject to the enslavement by inherited and otherwise acquired neurological, cognitive, and psychological programming? (For detailed discussion of this matter, see again Volume 6 in this series, titled, OVERRIDING THE EXTINCTION SCENARIO, PART TWO.)

**BREAKING THROUGH
THE SHACKLES OF OUR PROGRAMMING**

These are questions more readily asked than answered. Yet, we might move toward an inkling of an answer if we reflect upon the degrees of freedom allowed us by our biology and our brain's wiring. Consider the view that we function on genetic and neurological automatic the majority of the time. We fool ourselves into believing that we exercise a great deal of free will. We may be in a state of programmed-in denial about our mechanical, robotic, programmed, and programmable nature.

We living things are creatures of habit. As has been explained in the previous chapters, our ability to biologically program ourselves for automatic responses is essential for survival. For example, speedy responses to danger save lives. If we had to take time to think through each of our rapid responses to urgent situations, we would probably die off.

We rely on our automatic behaviors to respond to physical events such as falling objects, red traffic lights, and other situations that demand quick responses. We also may respond automatically to seemingly less critical physical events or conditions such as hunger for a snack, a cold draft in the house, or a baby's cry. Some pieces of this behavior are genetically inherited and thus instinct-driven, and other pieces are the result of patterning acquired during day-to-day experiences.

So convenient and readily developed is automatic emotional and physical behavior that it merges unseen with the non-physical realms of human interaction and emotion.

ADVENTURES IN CHANGES, TRANSITIONS, AND DEATHS

Public and private feelings, and their expressions, are often manifestations of psychological and social patterns. It is difficult to discern exactly what proportion of an individual's behavior is attributable to the larger social and cultural environment, and what proportion is particular, idiosyncratic to the individual.

It is also difficult to separate the larger social and political behaviors of the human population on Earth from the genetic programming nested within each cell of every individual human body.

Previous chapters have suggested that this ambiguity is especially obvious in blatant cases of explicit problem patterning such as drug, food, gambling, sex, danger/risk, and other addictions. Of course, much of this problem behavior blends in with overarching personal and social patterns. For example, so much of our cultural overlay is dedicated to the selling and feeding of food and at least legal drugs to the consumer. We are bombarded by advertisements to eat food, drink alcohol, and take painkillers. Is overconsumption, or addiction to these things, merely an individual malady? Or is this a population-wide acquired response to environmental stimulation?

Even if this question could be definitively answered, there is still the matter of our programming to automatically self-program into pattern addiction. Once a behavior, no matter what its origin, is repeated a number of times, a patterning program is eroded into the neural pathways that have repeatedly transmitted the biochemical message required to repeat the act.

The more repetition, the deeper the erosion -- the more wearing of pathways into the nervous and brain systems, and then the more automatic the behavior. The highly programmed and highly programmable biological robot within us rises, run by automatic programming, at once the prison and the prisoner here.

ADVENTURES IN CHANGES, TRANSITIONS, AND DEATHS

Meet the biological robot: You, me, everyone. Our life processes, our behaviors, our perceptions, our changes and transitions, even our death and dying processes, biological death itself being inevitable and appearing to be *the* final death, all appear to be so highly programmed into us.

Who or what wrote this script? Was this random evolution or some other force or factor? Will we ever know? And either way, our response must be an ever increasing awareness of what is taking place within and around us. We must strive to ever more consciously navigate our minor and major change, transition, and death processes.

DEATH AS ERASURE OF PROGRAMMING

There is no way, except perhaps physical death, to clear the mind-brain of all past impressions and programming. Those who believe in the spillover of experience from lifetime to lifetime will claim that even physical death is not a clearing. (For example, some trauma may be inter-generational.)

But let us say, for argument's sake, that physical, biological, death is an effective means of erasure, and that only this sort of death offers complete erasure. Biological death then may be a means of overcoming or transcending a problematic personal condition. Indeed, serious biological illness patterns can sometimes lead to death.

Or maybe, physical death is not a complete erasure but, instead, a sort of amnesia, allowing whatever it is that may live on when the biological body dies a chance to forget its biological programming. What a marvelous opportunity this might be for those who are deeply dissatisfied with the programming that they have either inherited or acquired. Yet, we cannot be certain that all deaths guarantee transcendence of programming. It is therefore as important to die well as it is to live well. Preparation for death is preparation for transcendence.

ADVENTURES IN CHANGES, TRANSITIONS, AND DEATHS

Again, this is _not_ an advocating of physical death as the only way out of problem conditions. Too many lives turn around, too many healings and recoveries take place, to believe that there is no way except physical death to escape unpleasant patterns. Physical death is merely one category of death along a continuum, or a matrix, of minor and major changes, transitions, and deaths.

Death, whatever form it may take, offers the opportunity for transcendence. [See again the path of pattern transcendence discussed in Chapter 5, with the four basic patterns being STRUGGLE, PARADOX, INSIGHT, and ELEVATION (spiritual elevation).] However, death or any transition for that matter, in no way guarantees this transcendence of patterns. Again, it is important to transition or die as consciously as possible, to die well so to speak, whether or not the death in question is biological.

BECOMING A SPIRITUAL REVOLUTIONARY

We may want to ask ourselves how far reaching, even intrusive and controlling, our programming is. Yes, much of the internal biological programming controlling us is life-saving and life-empowering, essential for our functioning biologically and psychologically – for our surviving as biological life forms. Yet, so much of this programming and its patterning processes are problematic and even harmful.

Programmed people are not free, they are in a sense biological robots (bio-bots) proceeding to function as programmed, obediently living the patterns they have been wired to form and live. Whatever bit of the actual SELF nestles within the heart of a pattern-operated and frequently problem pattern-addicted being may be on some levels trapped, stuck, caged, even suffocating in a paradoxical NO EXIT holding pattern.

What a double bind we humans face. We need this essential patterning function to live, to survive. Yet this

ADVENTURES IN CHANGES, TRANSITIONS, AND DEATHS

same function can kill us, and most certainly interferes with our survival of many a transition, including the ultimate biological death and dying processes. (For deeper discussion of this matter, refer to other books in this KEYS TO CONSCIOUSNESS AND SURVIVAL SERIES, such as the in depth discussion of the highly controlling and programmable brain functions, and of how these affect our survival both positively and negatively, in Volume 6, OVERRIDING THE EXTINCTION SCENARIO, PART TWO.)

Too many spirits allow themselves to be suffocated by largely invisible problem patternings, eventually permanently extinguishing themselves. Any Master Plan of the Cosmos that would have planned for this development, if you believe there is one, perhaps can and must be overthrown. Too many souls are being enslaved, turned into robots, lost. The massive stagnating and extinguishing of the free will of human souls threatens the perpetuation of any freedom within all Creation.

You become a sort of revolutionary when you master change, transition, and death processes – **when you learn to detect and where needed override programming -- including programming to die, to stop existing, when the biological body dies.** This is because the perceived limits to your reality, your prison walls, can be broken through by you applying the tools of ever heightened awareness.

ONLY A FRACTION OF YOUR REALITY

The world you believe you see is only a fraction of reality, if that. This means that what you perceive as a catastrophic development is only a fraction of reality, if that. What you are programmed to see as death is only a fraction of reality, if that.

Even in what may feel to be your darkest hour, when you may feel you have sunk to the depths of despair, when

ADVENTURES IN CHANGES, TRANSITIONS, AND DEATHS

you may feel you grovel at the very bottom of the pit of misery, when hope may seem to be nothing but a foolish memory, **you can manage to find the smallest thread of inspiration.** You can somehow discover the speck, the hint, of light in your atmosphere. This hint of light is there at the almost invisible end of this infinitesimally minute thread that dangles before you.

And this speck of LIGHT can be your lifeboat. You can find this lifeboat and ride this lifeboat to your survival here and BEYOND.

There are several understandings involved in liberating yourself from the confusion and fear of difficulties and disasters. These include the following knowings:

- The world you believe you see is only a fraction of reality, if that.

- This means that what you perceive as a challenging or even catastrophic development is only a fraction of reality, if that.

- What you perceive as death is only a fraction of reality, if that.

- Your feelings regarding challenging or even catastrophic events, illnesses, and endings are important. They reveal to you the degree of attachment, the extent of your cording, to the reality that you are seeing affected by developments.

To consciously navigate challenges and even catastrophic developments, you must continue to remind yourself of the above information -- and then ride the storm of your disaster, grab its reins and navigate your ride through this disaster, and use the energy of your experience to release you — to ascend you — **to transcend troubled patterning into a new reality.**

ADVENTURES IN CHANGES, TRANSITIONS, AND DEATHS

OUR SENSE OF LOCATION

Finding our way through struggles and their paradoxical situations, through challenges we may face, involves seeing or sensing where we are in our patterns and situations, and in the surrounding patterns and situations.

Our sense of location in place and time is key in our finding our way, in our not getting lost in the sea of internal and external patterns and processes. This location is an idea, a perception, a sense we give ourselves to hold ourselves together as we move through change, transition, and death processes.

GENERATE A SENSE OF INTER-DIMENSIONAL LOCATION FOR DIRECTION AND COHESION

This sense of location we can generate for ourselves can be a sort of internal compass. This compass can show us that what we see is a fragment of the whole picture – but a piece of our reality – even but a piece of our inter-dimensional reality.

BECOMING THE PHOENIX

Consider the popular mythology of the Phoenix, the bird who rises from the ashes, from the spoils, from the remains of an apocalypse, the bird whose egg is hatched in the heat of that mythological cataclysmic global fire and then rises in full splendor. The concept of the Phoenix rising can be you, you rising from the situation you are in, you transcending patterns that must die, you resurrecting your SELF, you surviving.

Most ancient mystics viewed the Phoenix as symbolic of the immortality of the soul. Initiates into mystery schools who were considered to have been reborn were raised to the level of what was often called "phoenix." Egyptian mythology describes what it calls the "Ka" as the Egyptian "bennu" or phoenix bird; Ka often appears to the deceased in the form of a blue phoenix, offering the recently

physically dead person (the "Ba," or lower self), the opportunity to rejoin her or his "Ka," or higher self, who is also the eternal mother. The shock and release of death can be seen as triggering this divine union and the uniting of the lower self with higher spirit.

Hold on to the vision of yourself as the Phoenix rising from the ashes. This can be the imagery of your own personal survival, the vision of your own personal transcendence or resurrection which can transport you – transport your own personal consciousness -- into your own personal ascension. Love yourself as the Phoenix. Always feel that this triumphant rising from the ashes can be yours. Embrace the Phoenix — this is you dying and surviving.

THROUGH THE PORTAL OF CHANGE

When you fully embrace change, transition, and death patterns and processes, you will know you have become

ever more aware and conscious of what you are experiencing.

You will set the captive free. You will fly through the portal of change into new worlds. You will rise from the ashes of challenge, transition, enslavement, and even seeming disaster, in splendor: the Phoenix transcending, the Phoenix resurrecting, the Phoenix surviving.

Every day, even every moment, you can be making the mind-shift that allows you to see in new ways your change, transition, and death processes. You can begin to see that you, your actual SELF, is who can survive both here and BEYOND. This is the greatest gift we can give ourselves: the truth about the SELF who need not die.

ADVENTURES IN CHANGES, TRANSITIONS, AND DEATHS

APPENDICES

PRIMER FOR LIFE'S MINOR AND MAJOR CHALLENGES AND PASSAGES

ADVENTURES IN CHANGES, TRANSITIONS, AND DEATHS

BOOKLIST AND RECOMMENDED READING: BOOKS, EBOOKS, AUDIOBOOKS, PROGRAMS

KEYS TO CONSCIOUSNESS AND SURVIVAL SERIES
by Dr. Angela Brownemiller

Volume 14
How To Die and Survive: Book Three
Key Insights, Messages, And Collected How To Die And Survive Concepts, Processes, and Exercises For Living, Dying and Surviving Here and Beyond

Volume 11
How To Die and Survive: Book Two
Extending Our Interdimensional Awareness: Next Concepts For Living and Dying
****

Volume 10
Seeing Beyond Our Line of Sight
Consciously Moving Through Life's Changes, Transitions, and Deaths
****

Volume 9
Navigating Life's Stuff–
Dynamics of Personal Change, Book Two
Keys to Consciously Moving Through Our Processes and Their Patterns
****

Volume 8
Navigating Life's Stuff –
Dynamics of Personal Change, Book One
Sensitizing to and Navigating Our Patterns and Their Processes

PRIMER FOR LIFE'S MINOR AND MAJOR CHALLENGES AND PASSAGES

****

Volume 7
Keys To Accessing The Beyond
Expansion, Elevation,
Transmigration,
Survival
Practices And Concepts

****

Volume 6
Overriding the Extinction Scenario, Part Two
Raising The Bar On The
Evolution Of The Human Species

****

Volume 5
Overriding the Extinction Scenario, Part One
Detecting The Bar On The
Evolution Of The Human Species

****

Volume 4
How to Die and Survive
Interdimensional Psychology,
Consciousness, And Survival:
Concepts For Living And Dying

****

Volume 3
Unveiling the Hidden Instinct
Understanding Our
Interdimensional Survival Awareness

****

Volume 2
Adventures in Change, Transition, and Death
Primer For Life's Minor And Major Challenges And Passages

****

Volume 1
Keys to Self

****

ADVENTURES IN CHANGES, TRANSITIONS, AND DEATHS

BOOKLIST AND RECOMMENDED READING
Continued….

Metaterra Chronicles Collection
Angela Brownemiller

Ask Dr. Angela Series
Angela Brownemiller

The Bloodwin Code (Episode Books 1, 2, 3, 4, 5)
Angela Brownemiller

Transcending Addiction
Angela Brownemiller

Gestalting Addiction
Angela Brownemiller

Contact us for information on the special
Science Fiction Series
on these consciousness and survival topics.
Email:
DrAngelaBrownemiller@gmail.com

PRIMER FOR LIFE'S MINOR AND MAJOR CHALLENGES AND PASSAGES

GET THE TRUTH ABOUT ADDICTION
Life-changing insights into the reality of patterns, habits, addictions, and obsessions in our lives and minds.

Now in powerfully narrated AUDIOBOOK as well as PAPERBACK and EBOOK forms!

SEEING THE HIDDEN FACE OF ADDICTION

Detecting and Confronting This Invasive Presence

Dr. Angela Brownemiller

SEEING THE HIDDEN FACE OF ADDICTION can be found on Amazon.com and DrAngela.com

ADVENTURES IN CHANGES, TRANSITIONS, AND DEATHS

VOLUMES 8 & 9 in the
KEYS TO CONSCIOUSNESS AND SURVIVAL SERIES

Can we better understand the journeys we travel through in our lives? Can we detect and work with the patterns and processes we are forming, living within, and moving through? How much can we see about the patterns we form, and sometimes feel we cannot change, are caught in? How do we sensitize ourselves to the patterning processes we are engaged in? Find your way through the maze of life. See:

NAVIGATING LIFE'S STUFF:
DYNAMICS OF PERSONAL CHANGE, BOOK ONE
Sensitizing to and Navigating Our Patterns and Their Processes

NAVIGATING LIFE'S STUFF:
DYNAMICS OF PERSONAL CHANGE, BOOK TWO
Keys to Consciously Moving Through Our Passages and Their Patterns

Now in Paperback, Audiobook, and Ebook forms.
Find these and other books by Angela Brownemiller on
Amazon.com and Audible.com and DrAngela.com

PRIMER FOR LIFE'S MINOR AND MAJOR CHALLENGES AND PASSAGES

Volume 10 in this
KEYS TO CONSCIOUSNESS AND SURVIVAL SERIES:
SEEING BEYOND OUR LINE OF SIGHT
by Dr. Angela Brownemiller

SEEING BEYOND OUR LINE OF SIGHT: CONSCIOUSLY MOVING THROUGH LIFE'S CHANGES, TRANSITIONS, AND DEATHS ... is a simple yet profound book offering subtle yet major shifts in the way we think about changes, transitions, endings, and deaths. Here, we can see that we have the capability of holding and empowering our conscious selves as we move through events, changes, transitions, even emotional, even physical, death processes. ... The journey this book takes us on opens doors to finding our way through challenging, trying, even very difficult, events and passages in our lives. ... That we can survive is central as we undergo all minor and major transitions in our lives. ... Find yourself, know yourself, guide yourself through the minor and major transition and death processes you face during your life. You can define who and what you are for yourself. You can open this option in your mind, the option that you can develop this knowledge of yourself, and then carry this knowledge of yourself through this life, and perhaps also on beyond this lifetime.

ADVENTURES IN CHANGES, TRANSITIONS, AND DEATHS

Ancient teachings, messagings through time and space,
Earth herself, are calling us now.

For more information on author
Angela Brownemiller's
mind-body-spirit-consciousness
concepts and processes
and her other work, see:
DrAngela.com

The works of **Angela Brownemiller**
are brought to you by:

METATERRA® PUBLICATIONS
(**and numerous other publishers**, see Amazon.com).
For copies of print books, audiobooks, and ebooks
by this author,
see
Amazon.com
or contact us at
DrAngela.com

To take part in our events and workshops,
and or
for personal consultations
in person or by telephone or online,
contact us at
DrAngelaBrownemiller@gmail.com

ADVENTURES IN CHANGES, TRANSITIONS, AND DEATHS

ABOUT THE AUTHOR
Dr. Angela Brownemiller
Dr. Angela®

Dr. Angela Brownemiller, also known as Dr. Angela®, is an author, journalist, social thinker, clinician, psychotherapist, trainer, speaker, and creator of the ASK DR. ANGELA Series of broadcasts, podcasts, books, audiobooks, Ebooks, and programs. The views of Angela Brownemiller are centered on the great potential of the Human mind, heart, and soul, and on the rights of all of us, who and whatever we are (or think we are). Dr. Angela Brownemiller views the Human consciousness as a wealth of opportunity for exploration, insight, knowledge—and survival.

DrAngelaBrownemiller@gmail.com
DrAngela.com

www.ingramcontent.com/pod-product-compliance
Lightning Source LLC
Chambersburg PA
CBHW060817190426
43197CB00038B/1836